# Big Sam's Guide to Life

# Big
# Sam's
# Guide
# to Life

**BLINK**
bringing you closer

Published by Blink Publishing
3.08, The Plaza,
535 Kings Road,
Chelsea Harbour,
London, SW10 0SZ

www.blinkpublishing.co.uk

facebook.com/blinkpublishing
twitter.com/blinkpublishing

Hardback – 978-1-911274-94-0
eBook – 978-1-911274-95-7

A CIP catalogue of this book is available from the British Library.

Designed and set by seagulls.net
Printed and bound by Clays Ltd, St. Ives Plc

1 3 5 7 9 10 8 6 4 2

Blink Publishing is an imprint of the Bonnier Publishing Group
www.bonnierpublishing.co.uk

*This book is dedicated to the wife, the men of the armed forces and Sir Alex Ferguson. Your belief in me is the very electricity that powers my magnificence.*

# Contents

# Prologue

Nineteenth October 1954. Dudley, West Midlands, England. A woman screams. A harried doctor wipes his soaking brow. He looks down again. He can see the woman is crowning.

'You're crowning, sweetheart,' he says cheerily. She doesn't respond.

The doctor has never seen a head as big as this before. As mighty. This one is special.

'Nearly there,' the doctor tells the woman, reassuringly. 'One more push and we're done.'

The woman obliges, and pushes with all her might.

'Jesus Christ,' she screams. 'It's like trying to crap out a medicine ball.'

Then, it happens. Shards of glorious light burst into the room, as angelic voices begin to hum from on high. As the rest of the world comes to a halt, the woman's glistening undercarriage opens like a flower. Admittedly like a rather battered flower. A final push and the future of English football slides out with grace. With swagger. With aplomb. The moment has finally arrived. It is beautiful. It is serene. It is Big Sam.

In the six decades that have flown by since that momentous autumn afternoon, I have carved my own place in the annals of football history. I have taken the talents that tumbled out of that vagina with me back in 1954, added a splash of cunning, a hint of charm and a few dollops of sports science innovation and established myself as one of the true greats of the modern game.

If there was a Mount Rushmore for British football managers, I'd probably be up there. Along with Sir Alex Ferguson, Sir Alf Ramsey and … Barry Fry, probably. He does so much for charity, that lad.

However, my domination of English football only tells half the story of my life. I have spent over 60 years on this planet, leading a rich, provocative existence. In that time, I have accrued a wealth of experience and knowledge across a plethora of topics, such as sex, art, politics, and how best to groom one's pubic region. I am a walking encyclopedia of wisdom. Wisdom that I haven't always been able to fully and directly dispense to my legion of admirers. Until now.

Within these pages you will find stories. Lessons. Life lessons aimed at equipping you with the kind of heavy armoury needed to traverse an increasingly challenging 21st century. Read these words and heed my message.

Open wide and let me wring the sponge of my perspicacity into your parched mouths. Swallow it slowly and thoughtfully, letting the cool, invigorating waters of my sagacity quench the thirst of your curiosity.

And make sure you pay full price for these messages, too. Don't be borrowing a copy from a friend or paying next to nothing for one off some prick on eBay. I've got fucking overheads.

# How to Deal With Betrayal

> *'Yet each man kills the thing he loves*
> *By each let this be heard,*
> *Some do it with a bitter look,*
> *Some with a flattering word,*
> *The coward does it with a kiss,*
> *The brave man with a sword!'*

Oscar Wilde wrote the withering words above in 1897, whilst in exile in France. He fled to the continent after spending time behind bars simply for being a gaylord. Just think about that for a second. All the wit and creativity he possessed, all the joy and love he gave to his fans, the consistently remarkable job he did in his chosen field. It all counted for nothing in the end and why? Because some nark didn't like the fact that big Oscar liked it up the biscuit aisle. What a fucking joke.

I, too, have been on the receiving end of such stinking betrayal. Back in 2016, I was honoured with a gift even more precious than freedom. After working towards it for my entire professional life, the title of England manager was finally bestowed upon my mighty head. Little more than two months later, however, this gift was cruelly ripped from my clutches, as I was forced to quit. Why? Because of double-crossing, sly-winking, sham-mongering charlatans, that's why. The fucking cunts.

On 4 September 2016 I took charge for what was to be my only game as England boss. A devastating 1-0 win against Slovakia in our opening game of the 2018 World Cup qualifying stage was enough to make the rest of the world sit up and take notice. England were back. Long gone was the flaccid, primitive football played by my predecessor, Roy Hodgson, to be replaced by a modern, decisive, pulsating approach, masterminded by the grit-caked jewel in the English game's crown – yours truly. Barry Fry described it as one of the most impressive wins he'd seen all month and said about me, 'This guy is to winning what Chinamen are to inventing stuff. Fucking dynamite.'

It may have only been one game, but after the utter misery of Hodgson's pathetic Euro 2016 campaign it was just the tonic the country needed. It enabled the people – my people – to dream once again. To be lost in reverie, fantasising about being able to take to the streets of London Town in July 2018 and welcome back the world champions. I alone did this, and how did they thank me? By conspiring.

For the ignorant amongst us, those who consume only the empty, unwholesome calories of tabloid newspapers, the story went thusly: drunk on my own newly found power, I attend a meeting with undercover reporters posing as Asian businessmen and proceed to tell them how it is possible to get around FIFA and FA bans on third-party ownership of football players. I am also seen using my position as England manager to negotiate a £400,000 deal to take on an ambassadorial role at the fictitious company the aforementioned businessmen are representing. Sound about right?

Sound about wrong, more like. Perhaps I attended that meeting simply to ensnare a couple of dastardly dickheads that were, as far as I was aware, plying their filthy trade in the game that I love? Doesn't that sound much more like me? While the spider was, indeed, trying to catch the fly, I have to be honest and admit that I also met with these businessmen for an altogether more selfish reason. Insurance.

Remember that bit in *Home Alone* when Marv was trying to break into the McCallister's house, but Kevin spotted him and started playing that terrific looking gangster flick, and Marv thought a VHS tape playing on a small TV in a kitchen sounded like actual people conversing a few feet away from him (because obviously his ears are made of fucking cloth). And then he heard one of them shoot the other and then Marv scarpers back to the van and he says to Harry, 'let's get out of here, Harry, some lad called Snakes just smoked some other cunt and we better go,' and Harry says, 'Whoa, whoa, whoa! What if the cops nick us for all these robberies and want to know about some murder we had nowt to do with, wouldn't it be good to have information on this Snakes lad that we can use as a bargaining tool?' And so they stick around and eventually they find out that Kevin definitely is home alone and the whole thing was just a scam on his part and Harry and Marv are both like, 'Well, well, well ...'

In many ways, that was very much how I approached the meeting. I wanted to catch these slugs in the act. I wanted to have first-hand evidence of their nefarious dealings so that, in the event that I needed some leverage with the FA at some point in the future, I'd have it in my back pocket. Oh, sorry FA bosses, I didn't make it to the quarter-finals of the 2018 World Cup? And I've told the toxic press to go fuck themselves rather than pathetically toe the party line like the last monkey in charge? And I dropped an E with Sammy Lee before my first training session with the squad? I've done all those things and now you want to sack me? Hmm, well, how about instead of that, I fill you in on a couple of dodgy Asians who are hell-bent on destroying this game from within with a heady mix of corruption and exploitation? Do you reckon that's a bit more important? You do? Oh, great. How about you go sort that that little mess out, then, and leave me alone to mould these soft cunts into a team that will conquer the fucking world?

That was the plan. Much like that daft prick Icarus, though, I flew too close to the sun and allowed its scorching heat to burn the wings of my nobility, melt the wax of my dedication and rip off the feathers of my ingenuity. Unsurprisingly, I then fell into the sea like a bag of dicks. The entrapper became the entrapee. How ironic.

I can still vividly remember the night I lost my job as England manager. I listened to Sun Kil Moon's *Benji* 14 times in a row, then phoned 999 and asked them to put my heart back together. But they couldn't. Nobody could. A mixture of duty and, yes, hubris had left me open to attack, and I was duped by a festering wound that continues to weep all over this beautiful game. Yes, those lads weren't actually dodgy businessmen, but dodgy businessmen DO exist. My actions may have been blind, but they were also sort of virtuous and brave, if you think about it.

The FA, however, choose to ignore this bravery and focus solely on the fact that I was caught on tape talking about how to circumnavigate their shit rules. The myopic turds refused to back me and that was that. After a mere 67 days, my time as manager of England was over. It was an act of betrayal that I will never forget.

One cannot, however, let betrayal trap you forever. One must use it as fuel, learn from it and let it empower you. I've been in this business for almost five decades and, believe me, nothing can nourish success quite like the embittered determination to get one over on some prick that has wronged you. The FA will rue the day they let this beauty queen slip out of their grasp. Just bloody see if they don't.

Unlike the tragic tale of Oscar Wilde, I bounced back from my betrayal reasonably quickly. While he spent his remaining years in impoverished exile, wandering the streets of Paris alone before finally succumbing to cerebral meningitis, I got a job at Crystal Palace, which isn't anywhere near as bad. To paraphrase the great Rocky Balboa, life is not always about how hard you can hit. It's about how hard you can get hit and keep moving forward.

Oh, and the £400,000 I accepted to take on an ambassadorial role at a fictitious company? Where did that fit into my plan to expose corruption? It didn't really. I just fancied £400,000. Oscar Wilde ended up walking around Paris like a fucking tramp. Not me, my friends. Mama didn't raise no fool.

# Puns

Tactical innovation. Grit-caked northern fortitude. A smile as cute as a dormouse's minge. Some of my strengths are there for all to see. Many of my most potent virtues, however, are not as widely recognised or cherished by the general public. One of these is my devastating ability to pun.

I've been a fan of punning since I was seven years old, when I took a trip to the beach with my great-uncle Bernie and witnessed him in action. Bernie was a real character and no stranger to a touch of devilment. Sadly, he also wasn't a stranger to consistent accusations of spiking cattle water troughs with bleach, but that's another matter entirely.

As I played with my sandcastle, Bernie began to get into an argument with a woman. A – some would say – rather aggressively gay woman. The woman, it transpired, had provoked Bernie's ire by not wearing a poppy. As the quarrel escalated, Bernie suddenly shouted, 'Lesbian havin' you!' before raining ferocious blows down upon her. It was pointed out to him afterwards that he had rather shoehorned the pun in by pronouncing it 'Lesbeen' and, perhaps more importantly, that wearing poppies in June isn't really the norm for any demographic, but he was having none of it.

Despite the trauma of seeing a man in his sixties assault a woman with a more precise crewcut than him, the incident ignited my love for playfully provocative paronomasia. I've amassed a treasure trove of cracking pun-work in the half-century since then. Here are some of my favourites.

**November 1993**: I'd had a short stint with the Tampa Bay Rowdies when I was a player and during my time over in the States, I became utterly fascinated by American Football. Fast forward a few years and as I beavered away as youth team coach at Preston North End, I decided to take a trip to Los Angeles to watch the LA Raiders play and to see if I could translate some NFL insights into Association Football. Long story short, I couldn't, so I spent most of the time eating prime rib and taking in the sights. On one particularly gorgeous morning, I took a stroll around the wonderful Griffith Park. As I tackled a rather rugged hiking trail and admired the glorious pink sunrise as it lovingly bathed my exposed torso in a sensuous, earthy glow, I spotted something from the corner of my eye. It was a person. A man, kneeling against a tree. A lovely old sycamore, to be precise. I got closer, and realised that I recognised him. It was none other than Ted Danson, star of hit sitcom *Cheers*, which had recently come to an end after 11 seasons of stellar laughs. As I crept up behind him, I realised that Danson was crying, and crying hard.

I found out after the whole episode that Danson was sobbing over the end of his romantic relationship with actress Whoopi Goldberg, star of *Sister Act 2* and *Sister Act 1*. It was all very well discovering this after the event, but I didn't know it at the time and, in my ignorant state, I approached the mourning mirth-maker with less than appropriate caution.

'There he is,' I bellowed loudly. 'Danson – with tears in his eyes.'

After what seemed like an interminable silence, he stood up and faced me.

'What?' he replied softly, rubbing his reddened eyes with shaking fingers.

'You know – that Ultravox song.'

'Who?' he asked, his voice getting louder and firmer.

'Midge Ure.'

'What?'

'"Vienna" was the other one, wasn't it?'

And with that, Danson was gone. He moved full-time into movies the following year, starting with *Getting*

*Even with Dad*, alongside a then still-hot Macaulay Culkin. It was shite.

**February 2002**: At the end of a four-day bender with Gary Wilmot, we ended up at Ronnie Scott's legendary jazz club in London Town. As we stumbled around the bar, Gary's eyes widened. He motioned towards a charmingly secluded little alcove in the corner, where then England manager Sven-Göran Eriksson was getting very fresh with a lady. Despite staring for a really long time, we struggled to identify the woman, Sven being draped over her like gravy on a pie. We could see, however, that she was a bouncy little blonde number and very much *NOT* Nancy Dell'Olio, the sensual, raven-haired Italian with whom Mr Eriksson was in a very public relationship.

Gary, who was filled with ecstasy pills and rum, became giddy at this stage and, at the top of his beautiful voice, implored Sven to 'give her the digitry'. The startled Swede peeled himself off his prey with a jump and flopped back onto the plush crimson sofa like a disgraced salmon. It soon became jaw-droppingly clear why he was looking so coy; the woman he had been pawing was none other than adorable actress Leslie Ash.

I'd always thought Leslie was lovely. 'You're lovely,' I tried to mutter to myself, but the alcohol had severely dampened my comprehension skills by this stage, so I ended up shouting it.

'You sly old Swedish dog,' smirked Gary.

'Dogs!' I shouted in potted agreement.

I looked at Sven. He looked every inch like a rabbit in the headlights. A child who'd been caught with his hand in the proverbial jar; a vagina-shaped jar at that. I gave him a reassuring wink. I wasn't about to land a fellow swordsman in hot water over what may well have been a minor indiscretion. 'Come on, Gary,' I said. 'There's nothing to see here. It's just Sven Behaving Badly.'

I ruffled Sven's hair and smiled at Leslie. Despite the awkwardness of the situation and the fact she was probably ruining the nation's favourite sporting couple, I was sure she would at least appreciate the cleverness of the reference. Instead, she just looked confused. She then turned to Sven and said something in Swedish. It was at that point that I realised it wasn't Leslie Ash at all. It was Ulrika Jonsson.

Ulrika looked really like Leslie Ash back then, I thought. Gary and I wished them well, made our excuses, and said goodbye. We left the club not long after.

**April 2013**: I was up a scaffold (don't ask) on Bethnal Green Road, when Bonnie Langford drove past in a huge, bright red Ford Transit van.

'Bonnie Long-Ford, more like!' I shouted. She didn't hear me and drove on.

As a side-note, there was a Calor Gas canister sat in every single passenger seat in the van. Not only that, but each one was actually tucked in with a seat belt. And Bonnie had a lit match in her hand. And she seemed to be screaming, 'I can do so much more than panto, but nobody will give me a chance!' Very peculiar indeed.

**May 2008**: After quitting my role as Newcastle manager, I decided to take a few months to find myself. I would eventually take up the reigns at Blackburn Rovers, but in the interim period I decided to do a bit of travelling.

My favourite destination was probably Sheffield. The people … the food … the culture. Everything I encountered just took my breath away. Full disclosure – my least favourite leg of the trip was, without question, Doncaster. Honestly, Syrian refugees would turn their nose up at that fucking shanty town.

Whilst in Sheffield, I took myself off to the Snooker World Championship. It was thrilling. I'd been a huge snooker fan ever since sitting, wide-eyed, mere inches from the television set, watching John Higgins win his second world title in 2007, beating Mark Selby 18–13.

I was in the crowd for the 2008 final, as the great Ronnie O'Sullivan took on Ali Carter. As Ronnie entered the arena to a crescendo of noise, I couldn't help but be swept away by the sheer energy of the occasion. Positioned just a few rows behind O'Sullivan's seat, I refused to let the opportunity pass.

'Hey Ronnie!' I shouted, as he took a cool sip of a clear, un-bubbled liquid that I assumed was water. He glanced towards me.

'Get Carter!' I roared, pumping my fist with vigour.

'Yeah,' he replied. And he did. He dicked the prick 18–8, and the rest is history.

I was on fire that night, and I knew it. Later on, I downed countless tequilas with Steve Davis, Hazel Irvine and John Parrott in a smoky little jazz club that was frequented by much of the snooker community. Steve spent most of the night cruelly taunting Dennis Taylor about the Troubles in Ulster, while Hazel kept banging on about Radiohead's *Kid A* album and how 'expansive and challenging' it was, despite the fact it was over seven fucking years old by that stage. Parrott couldn't handle his liquor and was in a pitiful heap by 11 pm. By midnight he was lying on a pile of coats in the corner, rubbing his belly and mewling like a stricken cat. Inevitably, he vomited everywhere. As Hazel and I headed for the exit and into the back of a waiting taxi, I stopped and looked down at the chubby Scouse mess with distain. There he was. John Parrott. Being sick. He was John Parrott, and he was sick. I couldn't resist. I leaned in and tapped him on the shoulder. He looked back at me, shaking like a shitting mule.

'You're snookered, pal,' I quipped.

And with that, I swept Hazel into the waiting taxi and back to my 3-star hotel. I was eating orange Match-makers out of her arse by dawn.

**December 2012**: During my time at West Ham, I, along with a few other club legends, visited a hospital for sick children over the Christmas period to spread some festive cheer and hand out cheap, tax-deduct-ible gifts. Towards the end of the afternoon, former Hammers hardman Julian Dicks began tucking into a selection box that was left over. My eyes narrowed as I watched him devour the candy with repugnant relish.

'I like Mars bars,' he slobbered, as he shoved one into his already-frothing gob.

'Snickers ain't half bad either,' he chortled, as he chomped it to pieces. 'They used to be called Marafons. Then they changed.' A pale child with no eyebrows, who was sitting within earshot, actually rolled his eyes at the sheer banality of it all, but it didn't stop Jules. 'Milky Ways used to be a different colour inside,' he mumbled as he swallowed the fucking thing whole in a single gulp. 'A bit like London, eh?' The pale child looked away in embarrassment.

I continued to watch, waiting for my moment, like a patient, muscular jaguar waiting to pounce on some unsuspecting queer of an animal that's about to have his face, body and arsehole chewed into fucking mush. Then it happened. He picked up another bar of chocolate. The one I had been waiting for: 'Don't really like these, but I'm balls deep now, ain't I?' he cackled, chocolate and saliva converging to form an unholy brown puddle just above where his chin should have been. As bits of biscuit and caramel flew through the air, I knew it was time to strike.

'Julian Twix!' I roared. I had to wait a full 11 minutes for the portly left-back to tackle that particular confectionery and open the way for my verbal assault but, when it happened, the rewards were immediately obvious. It was gold.

'Like the chocolate bar!' chuckled Trevor Brooking. 'He's done you there, Jules.'

And I had. I fucking well had. Sadly, at the exact moment I spoke, the pale, eyebrow-less child collapsed, and everyone ran to his aid. My wordplay that day never really got the attention or credit it deserved, but I didn't mind. I was able to enjoy it and that was all that mattered.

As I sat back and watched panicked nurses trying to tend to the sick child while simultaneously trying to ward off a confused Don Hutchison, who was determined to administer the Heimlich manoeuvre on the kid, I sat back and rested my mighty head on my hands, like some modern-day Ferris Bueller, resplendent in an ambitious plan coming to glorious fruition. 'Life moves pretty fast,' I whispered, to nobody and everybody at once. 'If you don't stop and look around once in a while, you could miss it.'

The child sadly died 36 hours later. He was pale for a reason, it seems.

As these examples show, a successful act of punnery needs patience, guile and, most importantly, an impeccable sense of timing. If you can master all those things, a whole world of delicious opportunity is ripe for your plucking. As my great-uncle Bernie used to tell me, as we watched cow after cow falling down in that big field behind his house: 'You can have it all, son. You can be a jack of all trades and a master of pun.'

# Three Steps to Seduce Any Woman

'A woman is much like a banana milkshake, son. Thick, unhealthy and disgusting.'

My dear friend Howard Wilkinson whispered those words to me in the summer of 2001, as we sat on the deck of his luxury yacht, *Howard's Way*, looking out over the beautiful, pristine waters around Zante. 'Snakes with tits,' he added, dispassionately, before taking a sip of his Hemingway Daiquiri and fixing the Ionian Sea with the coldest, deadest stare I've ever seen from a Yorkshireman.

Despite my fondness for Howard, and his hairline that looks a bit like the crest of a magnificently powerful wave, I certainly do not share his mistrust of the female form. I dig chicks. I dig their vibes, their auras, their soft, malleable flesh. Women adore me, too. Over the years, I've laid down with some of the most sophisticated broads in the history of British light entertainment. Rantzen, Turner, Greene, Pollard.

These delights and more have fallen under the seductive spell of yours truly. All consensual too, I should add, in case one of those fucking Yewtree busybodies is perusing these pages looking for a fresh new lead.

As a swordsman of particular clout, I've often been asked to share my secrets with younger studs looking to enchant the fairer sex. It's a tough ask; this kind of wisdom is not something I believe is possible to fully impart in easily digestible soundbites. As with so many things, experience is key. The adroitness of my cajolery is a direct result of over 45 years of sexual allure. Almost a half-century of temptation, enticement, beguilement and sexual magnetism has given me the tools to succeed, and I wear these skills as plumage. What I can do, however, is dispatch a few nuggets for your delectation; a few simple universal truths that I believe can aid the art of seduction. Nay: *will* aid the art of seduction. I'll just narrow them down to the top three, though. I haven't got all fucking day.

Leave your preconceptions at the door, dear reader. Forget everything you've ever been told, fix your lips to my nips and suckle. Suckle at the very milk of venereal sapience.

**Chivalry**: in a world of vulgarity, a demonstrative sense of gentility can set the gentleman apart from the scoundrel. The modern woman is beset on all sides by drooling, lascivious beasts intent on securing her flesh for their own filthy desires. Instead of sexting, why not compose her a sonnet? Instead of polluting SMS airwaves with pictures of your engorged tadger, why not stand beneath her bedroom window and play an agreeable pop hit from your boombox like the criminally underrated John Cusack in *Say Anything*? A simple show of courtesy can allay her fears and leave her like putty in your hands. How far should one go to reassure a lady about the wholesome content of your character? As my old uncle Enoch used to say, it's never enough if you want that muff.

**Confidence**: women are delicate and, because of this, men should be the opposite. Chicks don't want a foppish wimp who's too busy updating his Instagram with pictures of fucking sunsets to offer her the protection she needs in a 21st century teeming with villains, vagabonds and turbo-nonces. A confident man is a trustworthy man. Back in the late 1980s I took the great Gwyneth Powell out for a late lunch. Gwyneth is an English actress best known for her portrayal of headmistress Bridget McClusky in the BBC television series *Grange Hill* between 1981 and 1991. What you probably don't know about is the sheer power of her sexual zeal. It was legendary within the tittering halls of Television Centre. As we exited the cafe, a group of street-punks recognised her and approached. 'Hey, McClusky,' one of them sneered. 'What does Mr Bronson's bell-end taste like?' Gwyneth was appalled. And frightened. I sensed it immediately and, before the foul-mouthed hooligan had a chance to cackle at his own wretched taunt, I whipped from my pocket a pink snooker ball (any colour is fine, btw) tucked inside a cotton, pale-blue Geoffrey Beene handkerchief and cracked it at speed into the side of his skull. As he went down amidst a cacophony of agonised squeals, Gwyneth looked at me with stunned adoration. 'You're getting the full Powell treatment tonight, squire,' she purred. And I did. By Christ, I did.

**Dress to Impress**: Joseph Merrick was the legendary 'Elephant Man' of London Town. Known for his gentle heart, his unwavering belief in the human spirit, and his big conker head, Merrick was a true hero for disfigured, disabled lads everywhere. Picture him now. Go on. What does he look like? A face like cauliflower glued on to a half-deflated space hopper? Perhaps. An arm like a massive sausage? Maybe. But what is he wearing? That's right. A tuxedo. Merrick made an effort with his duds. Remember when he went to the theatre? The fucking theatre? Despite the horror of his appearance, Merrick was resplendent in slacks, dinner jacket and dickie bow. He only had one good arm, remember. He probably had to start getting ready at 9 am, for Christ's sake. But he did it. And why? Because he had dignity. Because he believed in looking as good as he possibly could, and you should too if you want to snare some poontang. Of course, Joseph Merrick wasn't able to seduce any women throughout his short life, despite his sartorial elegance. He died a virgin. And this despite the fact his penis remained untouched by his wretched disease and was, by all accounts, bigger than the Thames. A cruel, cruel irony.

I can't teach you everything I know in a few, short paragraphs but, if you follow these three simple tips, I am confident you can secure the woman of your dreams. Equip yourself with these weapons and you'll be slinging your proverbial arrows into her metaphorical dartboard in no time. Right into the bullseye.

# How to Thwart Disaster if Someone Plays Nickelback on a Pub Jukebox

et's make no bones about it; Phil Brown is one of my very best friends. He's been a pupil, a colleague, a comrade and a confidant. He's been with me through thick and thin. When I lost my job at Newcastle United, he ran me a big bath and made me liver and onions for tea. After tasting defeat to Middlesbrough in the 2004 League Cup final, he let me borrow his favourite whore – a dusky, enchanting mistress known colloquially as The Shadow. When I was framed by elitist charlatans, who broke my heart and cost me my dream job with England, he sat by my bedside, plucking his Spanish guitar and soothing me with the most beautiful rendition of 'A La Nanita Nana' that I have ever heard. For anyone wondering, it's a truly gorgeous little Spanish lullaby and one of my favourite tracks of all time. The lyrics, when translated into English, are quite exquisite, and illustrate just how much Phil *gets* me.

*Come, let's sing a little lullaby*
*Come, let's sing a little*
*My baby girl is sleepy*
*Blessed be, blessed be*
*Little spring running*
*Clear and loud*
*Nightingale that in the forest*
*Sings and weeps*
*Hush, while the cradle rocks*

As I lay there, tears snaking through the granite contours of my face and jaw, his words and melodies pulled me back from the brink.

'You are my Lancelot,' I said, touching his cheek with my big finger and smoothing his chin with my thumb. 'And I am still your king. I love you, Phil Brown.'

'Ditto,' he replied with a wink, before launching straight into 'Unchained Melody'. Gluing my heart together, whilst still having the time to make dead clever pop culture references? I'm telling you, this cunt is good.

Phil does, however, have his flaws. As a football tactician, he's shit. Like *proper* shit. When we were at Bolton Wanderers together he tried to convince me to sign a lad solely because he had a club foot. 'Look at his big, twisted tootsies, boss,' he said, pointing towards this unfortunate creature that he had dragged off the streets and into my office. 'Think of the bend he'll get on set pieces with that thing.'

His most egregious feature, though, is probably his temper. I can be hot-headed, sure, but I've never seen anything like Phil when he truly loses his rag. A few years ago, when a disabled fella on a mobility scooter cut him off in a Tesco car park, Phil yanked him off his vehicle by the hair and chucked him into a nearby canal. I can still see the poor fella's little withered legs spinning towards the water like a pair of trembling turkey wattles.

A very easy way to push Phil's buttons is to offend his musical sensibilities. Browner is a serious music buff. He's got all the *Now That's What I Call Music!* albums on tape and has seen Del Amitri in concert 47 times. Yes, he's a bit of a hipster, but he has an appreciation of the art that I've rarely encountered with any of my backroom staff.

In October 2001, Nickelback's execrable 'How You Remind Me' swept the airwaves like a devastating flood swarming over an ill-prepared Asian village. It was a truly dreadful song, and the singer looked like a Crufts runner-up that had been put through a tumble dryer. Unsurprisingly, Phil hated it. 'I hate this!' he roared, as it blasted out of the jukebox in the Finishers Arms pub in Bolton.

'Settle down, Phil,' I retorted with clarity. 'This is a friendly, traditional pub with a great range of cask ales. It's listed in the CAMRA *Good Beer Guide* and its affordable pub menu provides a great selection of home-cooked meals and a traditional Sunday lunch. Just relax.'

It was too late, however. Phil had already made a beeline for the person at the jukebox who was responsible for this aural massacre; a tall, thin man in his early twenties, decked out in a leather waistcoat and earrings in BOTH ears.

'Fuck are you doing?' seethed Phil.

'I beg your pardon?' the thin man replied. Big mistake.

'Phil Brown don't beg for no man.'

'Sorry, I ... I don't follow you.'

'You'll follow me into the gates of hell if you play that shite again.'

'Look, I don't want a problem, mate. I'm just here because of the cask ales. Did you know this pub is listed in the CAMRA *Good Beer...* '

'SHUT THE FUCK UP, YOU LANKY SLUT! Play that shite again, and I. Will. End. You.'

With that, Phil backed away from the jukebox and returned to our table, maintaining eye contact with the thin man for the entire journey. The tension in the pub was palpable. A family of four that were sat at a nearby table looked on in terrified silence. The thin man was shaking visibly. He must, however, have had a touch of Dutch courage inside him – perhaps a few pints of the

Blackedge Pike, a really pleasant pale ale with plenty of citrus sweet hop aroma – because what he did next can only be attributed to the madness that alcohol can provoke.

The thin man looked back at Phil, who had sat down but still wouldn't break his apoplectic stare, before smirking and taking a 50 pence piece out of an admittedly adorable little chest pocket on his waistcoat. As his smirk widened, he carefully, and rather dramatically, placed the 50p into the jukebox. 'Please be Limp Bizkit this time,' I thought, although, as is often the case when I'm stressed, I actually shouted this out loud instead of thinking it to myself. The thin man looked at me and shook his head. His long, slender fingers moved slowly towards the buttons on the jukebox. As he plunged in his selection, I closed my eyes. I closed my eyes and I prayed. The jukebox whirred into action. Then, silence for what seemed like an eternity. Then... Nickelback. That bastard opening line seeped filthily out of the speaker, like diarrhoea dripping out of a sickened anus.

Before I could even look towards him to gauge his reaction, Phil had crushed the pint glass in his hand, with shards of glass and pools of Thwaites Wainwright – a delicious, invigorating and refreshing beer, made with a unique combination of hops and 100 per cent Maris Otter malt to provide subtle sweet notes and a delicately citrus aroma – flying through the air. He tossed the table aside like a shit orphan.

'FOR QUEEN AND COUNTRY!' he bawled, before charging head first into the thin man.

As the appalling lyrics and workmanlike guitar chords grew louder and louder, the thin man's head sank devastatingly into the glass of the jukebox. As his skinny frame went limp, Phil reached in and ripped out both of the lad's earrings. Blood squirted through the air as the thin man screamed in agony. Jesus Christ, the screams.

'It's not a good song!' Phil howled, before lifting up the poor lad and suplexing him viciously through the family of four's table with a thundering crash.

As the children began to wail, and their parents shrieked in panic, and that dreadful fucking chorus somehow began to pour out of that now-destroyed jukebox, I knew I had to act. I rushed towards Phil, who by this stage had taken off his shoe and sock and rammed his tanned foot into the thin man's quivering gob. He'd pushed it in as far as the ankle by the time I arrived. Instinctively, I pushed two of my fingers into Phil's nostrils and hooked him by the snout; my great-uncle Bernie hunted pigs and as a boy I had learned how to subdue the beasts as Bernie worked on them with a snooker cue. I pulled Phil towards me. He was frothing at the mouth by now and looking like a proper fucking mentalist. I'd managed to peel him off the slain juke-box-bothering prick, but I knew I couldn't keep him static for long, this cat has the strength of a mentally disabled adolescent when vexed. An idea suddenly pinged into my head: 'A La Nanita Nana' – our shared Spanish lullaby. I pulled him towards me, until his forehead pressed against mine. My eyes rolled back to white.

*Fuentecita que corre clara y sonora*
*Ruiseñor que en la selva*
*Cantando y llora*
*Calla mientras la cuna se balancea*
*A la nanita nana nanita ella!*

Little well running clearly and profoundly
Nightingale in the jungle
Singing and crying
Getting quiet when the cradle is rocking
To her the little, tiny girl

The anger in his eyes evaporated, like at the end of *An American Werewolf in London* when pretty nurse Alex tells her lupine beau, David, that she loves him. In that film, the serenity that comes over David is only fleeting and he soon leaps angrily at Alex before being torn apart by police gunfire. My lullaby, though, had tranquillised Phil completely. His head rested on my shoulder and he began to sob.

'Is he dead, boss?' he slurred, ropes of his snot dangling against my Ted Baker wool twill jacket. I kicked the thin man. A low groan emitted from his mangled face.

'No, son. He might need a ramp to get in here the next time he fancies a cask ale, but he's very much alive.'

And with that, I lifted Browner into my arms, like a monkey, and carried him out of the pub. We had ordered lunch, and it was a shame to leave before it arrived, as the place really does have a great selection of freshly-made specials that are ever changing, but it was time to go. As we headed to the door another tune sprang into life on the jukebox. It was 'Always the Last to Know', the effervescent 1992 hit by Scottish punk band Del Amitri.

'Del Amitri! squealed a suddenly sprightly Phil. 'It's Del Amitri, Dad!'

'I know it is, honey.'

'I like them.'

'I know you do, Phil Brown. I know you do.'

As I carried him towards my pristine 1938 BMW R61 motorcycle parked outside and placed him gently into the adjoining sidecar, I ruffled his hair and told him that I loved him. For it is love, dear reader. It is love that can quell even the most raging fire. Love washes over the bubbling volcanoes of anger and restores a cool placidity in even the most caustic of environments.

As an interesting side note, I once met Justin Currie, the lead singer of Del Amitri, at a Star Trek convention in Brighton, and told him this story.

'Mad,' he said, with the fakest fucking laugh you've ever heard in your life. Then he went off and stood in line to meet the fella who played Worf. An hour in line to get your photo taken with fucking Worf. What a bell-end.

# What to do When There's a Sex Scene on the Telly and You're Watching With an Elderly Relative

Halloween night, 2007. I return from trick-or-treating with a sumptuous haul.

'Look what I got!' I squeal as the wife opens the door to greet me. 'I got M&Ms and I got Refreshers and I got Bounty bars and I got Opal Fruits!'

'You got lots didn't you, honey?' she beamed, pride creeping across her face like the thick fog that seeped through the back streets of London Town, cloaking the crimes of Jack the Ripper as he terrorised whores with the blade, back in the year 1888.

'My little monster,' she added, patting me on the bottom as I raced excitedly into the living room to devour my plunder.

Mother was there when I arrived, sunk into her usual chair like discarded bubble gum stomped into the pavement. She'd had a fall a few weeks previously and was staying with us. Our relationship has always been strained.

'Fat poof,' she muttered as I ran into the room and poured the candy out of the black medical bag and onto the floor with barely concealed glee. I heard her but, as usual, I bit my lip and said nothing. 'Who are you supposed to be?' she snarled, looking at my costume with disdain.

'I'm Saucy Jack, m'lady,' I replied, tipping the brim of my top hat with a wink and trying desperately to inject some much needed levity to the proceedings.

'John Barrowman?' she replied.

'No, mother. I am ... the Ripper!' I stood up and swished my cloak dramatically.

'Yorkshire? I had sex with him, you know.'

'You had sex with Peter Sutcliffe?'

'Think so.'

I looked back at my candy with a sigh. Suddenly it didn't look so appealing. Nobody knew how to obliterate my appetite quite like Mother.

Later that evening, we sat down for a horror movie marathon. I've always been a huge fan of Halloween. The kitsch theatrics, the unsettling spookiness, the sense of impending dread. It's right up my street. It's probably why I settled in Bolton so quickly. Horror movies are a favourite of mine, too, and we had a veritable feast of spine-chilling tinglers lined up that night. *The Evil Dead, Fright Night, Mask.* We watched them all back-to-back as the missus and I tucked into my tasty

Halloween pillage. Mother was asleep for most of the evening, which was a bonus. Her dreadful, inert flatulence, however, was not. I'm convinced she followed through during *Fright Night*, but I've never been able to prove it, despite the cushion on her chair smelling like fetid dog dirt for days afterwards.

She finally roused herself as our movie marathon reached its pinnacle; *From Hell*, the 2001 Hughes brothers' chiller about Jack the Ripper and his reign of terror in Victorian-era Whitechapel. I've been fascinated by the Whitechapel Murders since I was a boy. Indeed, I've written a number of unpublished books about the identity of the person I believe was behind the famously unsolved crimes. The third in the series, *I Bet He Was a Jew or a Paddy* came closest to going to print, but the publisher backed out at the last minute, fearful of reprisals.

As *From Hell* began to get into its ghoulish stride, so, unfortunately, did mother. 'What's this shite?' she barked.

'It's called *From Hell*, Mother. It's about Jack the Ripper. I'm dressed as Jack this very night.'

'You look like Meat Loaf no matter what you wear,' she scoffed. Tears began to roll down my face, but nothing was stopping her now. 'Why do all the women in this have clean teeth?' she asked. 'Whores back then didn't have clean teeth. Your nan didn't have clean teeth.'

'Nana was a prostitute?'

'Think so. Loved a cock, either way.'

I stood up in anger, and yanked the video out of the Bush DVD/VCR combo player.

'Fuck this shit,' I roared. 'I'm dead into Jack the Ripper and you can't even let me enjoy a movie about him.'

'Who?' she said.

'JACK THE FUCKING RIPPER!' I yelped, my patience momentarily snapping. 'That's who I'm dressed as ... why the fuck do you think I'm wearing this shit?'

She didn't offer an answer. She didn't have one. Instead, she looked me dead in the eye, raised her right hip and broke wind for 17 uninterrupted seconds. When she was finished, a smug grin spread across her shrivelled face. 'One-nil,' she purred.

I looked away in disgust, and put the next movie on: *An American Werewolf in London,* one of the classics of the genre. I sat down heavily, the wife wiping my cheeks and slipping half a Caramac bar into my mouth to settle me down.

As the movie got going and David, the titular American, began to get into all sorts of bother on the Yorkshire moors, Mother proceeded to interrupt every few minutes with a litany of inane questions. She was relentless, and completely unperturbed by the fact that I didn't answer a single one.

'How did they not realise they were going off the road and onto the moors?'

'Why did they take him to a hospital in London? Don't they have hospitals in the north?'

'Will his shit look like dog shit when he turns into a werewolf and has a shit?'

I had reached the end of my tether, and was ready to explode, when the movie took a turn. After getting out of hospital, David goes home with nurse Alex, played with ravishing delectability by Jenny Agutter. As Alex shows David around her modest home, she tells him to make himself comfortable while she takes a shower. A devilish look flashes across his American eyes. Make myself comfortable? he thinks. How about I make myself a big, wobbly, American boner and bring it into the shower with me? The opening bars of 'Moondance' by the late, great Van Morrison begin to play. Uh-oh. It's crashingly obvious what's about to happen. We've got ourselves a sex scene.

Now, intercourse unfolding on-screen while you're watching with youngsters or the elderly is as painful an experience as one can suffer. The awkward eye-contact as everyone looks away from the screen. The sudden interest in one's shoes. The pretending to sit on the remote control so it changes channel and then intentionally taking forever to remember how to use the thing before finally turning it back. We've all been there.

With Mother, however, the discomfiture is ten-fold. Not because she's especially bashful in such circumstances. Quite the opposite, in fact. She absolutely fucking relishes sex scenes. Particularly if I'm in the room with her, for some reason. As David and Alex went at it in the shower, Mother sat up straight in her seat for the first time in about four weeks. Her eyes widened.

'She's about to get some uncut Yankee beef right in her fish pie,' she screeched, uncouthly.

I stabbed the inside of my cheek with my tongue and closed my eyes tightly in embarrassment. As the cinematic coitus reached the bedroom, Mother was almost drooling.

'Oh, Christ,' she moaned, 'Oh my fucking Christ, that looks fucking class.'

I tried in vain to keep my eyes fixed on the television and away from her, but with each repugnant wail that emanated from her direction it became increasingly difficult. Finally, I cracked.

'Good grief, Mother, will you get a hold of yourself?' Unfortunately, I soon realised, that was exactly what she had done. As I looked towards her, my face drained of blood. Vomit threatened to come up my gullet and drench the Drumstick lolly I was gnawing. It was a moment I shall never forget. As she sat in the same room as her son and his loyal wife, watching one of the most accomplished horror/comedy hybrids of the 1980s, my mother had started masturbating.

The Drumstick fell out of my mouth and crashed to the floor with a thud that sounded for all the world like the jet planes crashing into those tower blocks in New York on that fateful day in 2001. My eyes dropped to see her hand plunged into her velour tracksuit bottoms – she didn't wear underpants – and straight into her vagina. The vagina that had given birth to the leading tactical mind of his generation was now being treated like some sort of perverted cheese grater. It was horrendous. The act may have only lasted about 30 seconds, but it felt like hours. I've never seen any part of her body move so fast. It was like watching E. Honda from *Street Fighter II*, but instead of giving the Hundred Hand Slap to Ryu or that Indian lad with the massive limbs, she was doing it to her wispy old muff.

As she finished – and believe me, she fucking finished – she looked straight at me. As sweat dripped from her flaky forehead, she took her hand out from her trackie bottoms and placed it calmly on her lap, before lifting her right hip and breaking wind once again. 'Two-nil,' she said with a cackle, before cocking her head back and howling like a werewolf. A deranged, filthy, out-of-control werewolf. As quickly as it began, it was over. She closed her eyes and returned to the deep slumber she enjoyed for approximately 14 hours per day.

Mother returned to her own home a few weeks later. We burned the chair a few days after that. I haven't watched *An American Werewolf in London* again since, and I don't think I ever will.

If you find yourself trapped in a room with an elderly relative, as lovemaking breaks out on the TV, just get out. Don't bother with any excuses or worry about how it may be perceived. Just get out of the room and stay out. It's the safest option. The only option.

There's still something morbidly compelling about the case of the Whitechapel Murders and the fact that, well over 100 years after the crimes, we are still no closer to knowing the true identity of Jack the Ripper. Who was this beast, and what drove him to commit such wretched acts? Fuck knows. Perhaps he too was forced to watch his mum fingering herself from a distance of about four fucking feet.

# Band Names For Sale

Without wanting to sound like one of those wet, reality TV spunk-weasels that infest our screens every winter – with their stories about dead parents and the indignity of being forced to work a normal, nine-to-five job – music has been in my blood since I was a boy.

I was 13 years old in 1966. That year, The Beatles released *Revolver*, Bob Dylan dropped *Blonde on Blonde*, and The Beach Boys came out with their undisputed masterpiece, *Pet Sounds*. On a sunny summer afternoon, I entered Vibes, my favourite record store in Dudley and bought all three. Together, they carved out an experimental musical landscape in my young, impressionable mind that is still hungry to this day.

'Deez jams gon' make you feel a-right,' said Pepper Ray, the owner of Vibes, when I made my purchase. Pepper wasn't Jamaican. He was actually an exceptionally white former estate agent from Coventry who began speaking in a semi-Caribbean accent a few years earlier, after his marriage ended, and he suffered a complete mental breakdown.

'Wagwan, little Sam?' he'd say, every time I'd enter the store.

'Irie, irie,' I'd reply, with a knowing smile.

His pretend, knitted dreads were a little strange, but Pepper Ray was essentially a harmless, enthusiastic guy. He insisted I buy those records that day and, in doing so, changed my life. I ran home and played them back to back, and my musical sensibilities flattened and expanded as each new track seeped into my earholes. Within a week, I had started a band with a couple of guys who lived near me. We were called Ham Slice, and we fucking rocked. We incorporated everything from psychedelic rock to alt-country and back again. Sadly, our bassist Jax, a 40-year-old hospital porter who claimed to have fingered a pre-fame Janis Joplin on a 'work trip' to San Francisco, got nicked for stealing medical supplies, and we soon dissolved.

Ham Slice didn't achieve much, but our short time together cemented my love of music and confirmed the unparalleled thrill of being in a band. I formed dozens of bands in the years that followed. None of them got very far – although Kermit's Hermits Learnit D Hardway, a jazz-rock fusion group I formed in 1987, did support UB40 at the Hare & Hounds in Birmingham – but that was never the point. Being in a band was never about success and fame. It was about freedom, and expression. And getting more muff than Tony Blackburn.

While it may sound odd, one of the things I most enjoyed about being in a band was actually coming up with a name. I seem to have an uncanny knack for picking the perfect name for whatever musical vehicle I'm pursuing at any given time. I really don't know why; I guess I just have an instinctual feel for conceiving names that evoke the style, vibe and politics of the group in question. The fact I've had quite a lot of practice coming up with these names doesn't hurt either! Hahaha. Remember earlier when I said I went on to form dozens of bands after Ham Slice? That's what I meant by that joke there.

Choosing a band name is a pretty big deal. You can be provocative or pleasing, esoteric or obvious. But you must get it right. Some acts are blessed with oodles of talent, but a poor choice of moniker has ruined any chance they might have had of being taken seriously. Er, hello, Hootie & the Blowfish.

Choosing a band name is an art and it's very rare that you'll get it right the first time around. For every band I formed, I had about five or six possible different options for a name in my back pocket. As a result, I have created hundreds of band names over the years that have been left idle and unused. Until now!

Below is a select list of some of my favourite, mint condition band names, available at £49.99 per name – or three for £149. Take out all the stress of coming up with the perfect name for your band and let me do it for you. I've even broken the list down into genres, making it super easy to know which names will perfectly encapsulate your band AND your jams.

Just make your selection and email me at bigsamsfreshjams@hotmail.com for further instructions. I'm still in the midst of a lengthy dispute with PayPal, but you can transfer funds with Xendpay, Gonja DK or Xoom. Don't delay your quest to be the next Bon Jovi, Blues Traveler or Reef. Get your perfect band name ... TODAY!

## Rock

- Equilatard
- Bionic Quim
- Delicate Assault
- Online Content
- Badly Handled Divorce
- Back-Alley Break-In
- The Queer Shoes
- Dear Tree Bar Low
- Brunch?
- Dead Kidz

## Funk

- Wankk 2 Completion
- The Biscuit Aisle
- Pink Innards
- Creepin' While U Sleepin'
- Ooh, Right There
- Beef Curtainz
- Shove It Up Dat Pipe
- When's The Cutoff Point After Midnight In Gremlins

## Soul

- Honey, Nuts And Brown Sugar
- Best Wishes, Kate And Billy-Bob Thornton
- Forbidden Piggy Bank
- Vanilla Puddle
- Low Hanging Fruit
- A Blast O' Bovril
- Black Wives Chatter

## Jazz-Fusion

- Frankie Arsehole And The Nought Percent Finance
- Crimson Bedspread
- Marti Pellow, Is It Me You're Looking For? (perfect for a jazzy Wet Wet Wet covers band)
- Custard Creeeeeeeeem
- QwErTy BeRtY

- Momma's Got Ass
- The Babysitter's A Nonce

## Reggae

- Spiced Jerky
- Rum In De Tum
- MusLIMBS
- The Marijuana Cigarettes
- Sir Chobby Barlton
- Shit IMHO
- The Wet Wipes

## Punk

- Nazi Theme Park
- The Cock Sockets
- Fuck Pigs
- 2 Cats 2 Dogs 2 Bats 2 Hogs
- Pre Cum
- Thatcher's Snatch
- Vulgar Vincent And The Victims of Negligence
- Queef Richards
- Christians on Facebook
- Cunt Punch

Please don't delay – make your selection, email me at bigsamsfreshjams@hotmail.com and your journey to stardom could begin today.

I can also offer bespoke solutions for all your band name needs. If any of the above names don't quite fit your project, don't panic! Simply send me a brief description of your band, and what kind of sound you're going for, and I'll tailor a moniker that suits your vibe down to the ground. Just like I did for Menswear.

Email bigsamsfreshjams@hotmail.com ... TODAY!

# What if You Don't Realise Your Dreams?

All men need occasional guidance. You can have all the physical tools to unlock any metaphorical defence, but sometimes you just need to stick your hand up, like an underprivileged school child who has just soiled himself in class, and ask for help.

Back in early 2011, mere months after I was viciously sacked by Venky's – the deeply foreign owners of Blackburn Rovers – I knew I was in trouble. My behaviour became ever more erratic as I sunk into a deep, depression-fuelled funk. How funky did I get? Well, I took a visit to Blackburn city centre one busy Saturday afternoon dressed up as an eagle and began swooping down on unsuspecting pigeons and eating them raw. I got through about six of the filthy little bastards before a local constable popped me into the back of his van and took me back to the station for a beef Cup-a-Soup and a chat.

Thankfully, this proved to be the nadir of my plight, and just the kick up the minge that I needed. I've always been a fiercely independent, introspective person, and I've coated myself in an impenetrable armour since I was a boy. I find it tough letting people in, you know? At that point, however, I knew I had no choice but to remove this sheath and expose myself to the enlightening fingers of another hand. It was this acceptance that led me to travel to Denver, Colorado, and seek spiritual nourishment from Chief Serendipity B. Hawkins of the Southern Ute tribe.

I had struck up an online friendship with Chief Serendipity a year earlier, after crossing paths with him in one of the darker, more sinister corners of the 4chan website. Initially, we clashed anonymously after he posted a rather offensive, photoshopped image of Arthur Scargill and Margaret Thatcher, but we soon put that behind us and became firm friends. As our kinship grew, we exchanged poems, recipes and loose, free-writing prose that would make little sense to the Bisto-chinned Neanderthals that make up the vast majority of the modern football fraternity, but it spoke volumes about how Chief Serendipity and I were beginning to feel about each other.

As I languished in unemployment, nauseated by a diet of Findus Crispy Pancakes, Albert Camus and the type of pornography that would make a teenage goth recoil in horror, I took the plunge and flew out to meet the man I was starting to regard as my spiritual guardian. I won't lie and say I wasn't apprehensive about the whole thing. I've met people from the internet before and been crushed with disappointment, while my treatment at the hands of Blackburn Rovers really put me off Indians for a bit. In spite of all this, I soon found myself meandering through the foothills of the Rocky Mountains, on the back of a donkey called Inigo, on my way to meet a real-life Native American chief.

To cut a long story short, Chief Serendipity was a cracking lad. He had a head like a block of wood and wore Hi-Tec trainers, but he was a genuinely good guy, with a vibrant, rabid wit and a wonderful sense of adventure. His advice was both ethereal and astute. I broke wind loudly during dinner one evening and, before I could offer my apologies, he turned to me with a smile and said, 'He who rides obliviously atop the winds of change, knows not where such winds will take him but can still seek solace in the journey and reap the fruits that lie in wait at the foot of his destination.' I mean, wow, right? I'd always considered Steve Bruce to be the most erudite person I had ever met, but this scamp was different sauce altogether.

One moment, however, sent an icy, debilitating shiver racing furiously down my spine, like Katie Hopkins running to an internet-ready device when a beloved celebrity dies. As we were meditating one morning, following a rather gruelling game of Hungry Hungry Hippos, Chief Serendipity reached out suddenly and grabbed my hand. He looked to the skies and screamed something both inaudible and terrifying while shaking his little turtle-shell rattle with all the violence of an Irish nun. The teepee suddenly fell silent.

'Do you want to play Kerplunk instead?' I asked. He didn't answer.

The chief bowed his head and continued to chant. At that point I felt he was summoning the spirits of a thousand years of tribal wisdom. As he lifted his head up slowly, his eyes met mine and a foreboding clarity descended upon his gaze. As he caressed my hand gently with one hand, he stroked my now-soaking cheek with the other. He then leaned forward, and whispered into my ear: 'I really don't think you're ever going to manage in the Champions League.'

I was incapacitated. My face had become cold and hot at the same time, just like when you text the wrong person something deeply inappropriate such as a picture of your scrotum pulled up and over your cock so it looks like a little bumpy spaceship or something. All of my insecurities flooded my brain at once. I wanted to destroy this lippy fucking Indian, but I somehow managed to restrain myself.

'I appreciate your candour, and I shall take it on board,' I said with a coquettish smile.

I stood up, thanked him for his hospitality and counsel over the previous three days and exited the teepee with a quiet grace that I am still immensely proud of. My composure did waver a little when I got outside, as I burst into tears and then set fire to Inigo the donkey, but I soon regained my poise, hitch-hiked a lift to the airport and boarded the next flight back to the UK. I never spoke to Chief Serendipity B. Hawkins again.

Each and every season, as I watch as the Champions League wagon roll arrogantly back into town, I think back to the words that were uttered to me in a modest teepee deep within the Rocky Mountains. And when I do, I wonder just how seriously I should heed the prophecy that was laid down before me that day. The Champions League is the pinnacle of our game, replete with more superstar blood and sweat than Chris Brown's angry knuckles. I am not part of that world, though. As Galacticos like Ronaldo prance down the wing like wondrous, tanned unicorns, I am forced to watch on from the solitude of my own home, eating Monster Munch and jotting down intricate tactical musings on a cheap Five Star Spiral notepad from Tesco. A notepad that will never be shared with anyone more important than the wife. And that sucks big fucking balls, people.

What lessons did I learn from this chapter? This chapter of my life, I mean. Well, perhaps my hitherto failure to guide a team into the Champions League has nothing to do with my ability or the environment in which I work. Maybe the fact that I am yet to be given a chance of managing a club that truly fits the sheer resplendence of my ability and tactical acumen is not some distressing indicator of my stature within the game, but rather a result of the forewarning I received that day from Chief Serendipity B. Hawkins. A curse, if you will. A curse that will haunt me forever, rendering my whims both futile and doltish. Is Native American perspicacity too powerful a force to conquer, even for someone as physically and mentally potent as myself? In all honestly, it is a pondering that I haven't truly got to grips with yet, but one I must constantly force myself regretfully to consider.

I shan't let it define me, though. Sometimes dreams can go unfulfilled. We can cry about this stark reality or we can endeavour to do something about it. We can rally against this mysterious, willowy mistress called fate and take her on at her own game. I know what camp I am in. As long as there is hot blood in my veins and fresh spunk in my ballbag, I will not go gentle into that good night. No, I will rise up instead and continue my quest to realise my dreams. I don't know what the future holds for me, but if I ever decide to manage again it will only be with a team in the Champions League. Will it be Liverpool? Real Madrid? LA Galaxy? Who knows. I'll take my place at the top table of the game, though. It is my destiny.

Chief Serendipity B. Hawkins was wise about many things, but he misjudged the sheer intestinal fortitude of this Sitting Bull from Dudley, and one day he'll see just how wrong he was. One day the whole world will see. And do you know what? I'll do it for Inigo. Setting fire to that donkey was a huge error on my part. Aside from the unnecessary barbarity of the act, I could have ridden that furry little bastard to the airport.

# How to Avoid Small Talk With People in The Goods And Service Industries

Small talk is shit. Sure, it has helped me through over 40 years of marriage, as well as countless meetings and League Managers Association (LMA) luncheons, but as a man renowned for no-nonsense, whip-smart, straight talking, I view the very act of trivial, non-functional conversation as an affront to my skills as a communicator and, indeed, a raconteur.

The worst form of small talk is that which is imposed on us by people we encounter when procuring goods or services. We place our trust in these people to drive us to our chosen destination, cut our hair, or serve us soy lattes. Trust is a precious gift, but it's not enough for this lot, it seems. No, instead of simply doing their job with a brief, insincere smile that we can both accept as part of the interaction, these invasive creeps see fit to sandbag us with impotent, aimless anecdotes and intrusive queries about our lives. It sickens me to my stomach and renders me speechless, quite frankly, that in the year of our Lord 2017, these feckless serfs still have the audacity to infer some sort of intimate relationship with upstanding members of the public simply because we are forced to reluctantly collaborate with them in order to pay for something we need.

I am not a rude man; ask anyone at the LMA and they'll agree. Yes, I could scream 'SILENCE!' as soon as one of these filthy-fingernailed commoners begins to flap their lips at me, but I don't want to hurt their feelings or cause a scene. Thankfully, though, there is another way to nip this agonising ritual in the bud.

I am a man of resolve. A man of keen, fox-like cunning and, over the years, I have developed a number of foolproof strategies that are guaranteed to block even the most wretched cases of forced small talk from spreading like tedious wildfire. Simply follow these suggestions and the next time you're compelled to interface with professional service providers, you can ensure that any sort of lengthy conversing will be avoided like a pervert at a waterpark.

## Taxi drivers

The dark lords of the small talk world. I'm pretty sure most taxi drivers live in some sort of fortified castle that is cut off from the rest of the world, because as soon as I enter one of their wagons, they begin chatting like their fucking lives depend on it. I don't even think they begin a new conversation with each passenger, they just continue from the point their ranting was forced to halt when the previous customer leaped out of the car and gulped in fresh air with a huge sigh of relief.

I got into a cab in Soho, London, a few months ago, and before I could say 'Club Pedestal, please,' the big, hairy oik driving the cab shouts, 'And her ribs weren't even broken or nothing so she were lying when she said she couldn't stand up and forget about it until my mum went home,' at me and proceeds to relay the second act of a story that, I fully believe, concluded with the murder of his wife.

There are a few topics that must be avoided at all costs when dealing with a taxi driver. These themes are like red rags to a bull and will simply set him off. Football, politics, Steven Seagal movies, tits. Bring up any of these and watch him pound you with his thoughts and opinions like a cunt on Twitter. Choose your opening gambit wisely, though, and you'll be sitting in awkward, glorious silence in no time. Here's a few of my personal favourites.

*'Nobody mourns for Henri Paul, do they? It's all Princess this and Dodi that. Nobody mourns for my Henri.'* (Start sobbing at this point.)

*'What you reading at the moment?'*

*'Never, ever suck cocaine up your arsehole, my friend. Just don't do it.'*

*'How does your meter work, pal?'*

*(While looking wistfully out of your window.)* *'Too many black faces around here for me. Too much dark drama.' (It should, however, be noted that this only works if your driver is a man of colour. If he's a white Englishman, uttering a sentence like this will merely earn you a fist-bump and a long Facebook-worthy rant about not even being able to call yourself English anymore.)*

*'Do farts have lumps?'*

## Coffee baristas

The world seems to have gone coffee-mad over the last century or so. According to Wikipedia, coffee culture 'describes a social atmosphere or series of associated social behaviours that depends heavily upon coffee, particularly as a social lubricant'. It goes without saying, then, that I view 'coffee culture' as being worse than pestilence. I do enjoy a cup of joe, however. A good, strong mug of the ol' java. Buying one, however? Well that's a different matter.

I was in a coffee shop recently, being served by a 6-foot 7-inch man who referred to himself as a 'coffee scientist'. 'I love to just experiment, you know?' he said, as I stared at his man bun with contempt. 'This town seems to be fuelled on coffee,' he added with a chuckle. We were in Nuneaton.

This is a tough one, though. Despite their pretensions, and the way they wear short trousers with white socks, coffee baristas are usually a friendly sort and their dedication to their job is to be lauded. Still, we don't want to chat with men wearing T-shirts with necklines that expose their chest now, do we? Hit them with some of these.

*'If you were a woman you'd be fucking gorgeous.'*

*'Aren't you a bit old for this?'*

*'It's like Starbucks for tramps in here. Quaint.'*

*'You're a bit sassy for a fatso, aren't you?'*

'The Walking Dead *is shite, isn't it?'*

*'I* will *have a great day. Once I've buried her.'*
*(Walk out backwards at this point, without breaking eye contact.)*

## Barbers

While taxi drivers are perhaps the exhausting purveyors of small talk, at least they offer opinions. Barbers, by comparison, seem to read their lines off cue-cards.

'Not working today?'

'Out this weekend?'

'Getting your hair cut, aye?

These razor-wielding dullards are the doyens of affected small-talk, and they must be stopped in their tracks. Here's how.

*'Just a number two all over, please. And no swastika on the back. Don't know what I was thinking last time.'*

*'Jesus! I can really feel the heat of your balls on my forearm. Do you like me?'*

*'Love that bottle with the blue liquid and all the combs in it over there. I've got a similar one at home. My wife's head is in it.'*

*'Any holidays coming up? Every day is a fucking holiday since I lost custody of the kids.'*

## Supermarket cashiers

It's a tough time for the supermarket cashier business. Self-checkouts continue to make the job ever more redundant, while those that remain face the growing temptation to leave their profession behind for an adult learning class. Thankfully for us, most cashiers seem to be completely dead behind the eyes and would rather eat their own fists than converse with a customer. There are others, however, that you need to remain vigilant with. If you see one looking at you, with a big, thick smile spread across their plump fucking face before you've even reached the checkout, you're in trouble. Here's what to say.

*'I'm just going to call you Bernie, OK? You look like a Bernie. Big Bernie!'*

*'Why the fuck are you wearing a tie? Is that ironic? Brilliant!'*

*'When you die, they should put a big conveyor belt in the church so they can get your coffin up to the altar nice and quickly.'*

*'I need to get fanny pads for the wife. Do they come in different sizes? I'd say you need a big one.'*

*'No, I don't have my own bag. I'd put it over your fucking head if I did. Haha. Only messing, Bernie.'*

## Foreigners

While they are not technically in the service industry, I'm adding them as a special bonus because I really feel like it's a problem we must get a handle on.

It's a reasonably easy one, mind. If Jurgen Splurgen, from fucking Cologne or wherever, comes up to you in the street when you're minding your own business and begins mumbling incoherently about directions or asks where all the museums are in Bolton, just let your eyes roll back into your head, like a great white shark when he's readying himself to attack, and shout, 'GET OUT!'

The more unholy you can make it sound, the better. Remember that scene in *The Amityville Horror*, when Father Delaney, played with aplomb by Rod Steiger, is attempting to undertake a blessing ritual in a bedroom of the cursed house and all these flies start appearing in the room, even though it's winter, and they're all over the priest and he's all, 'Jesus Christ, what's with the fucking flies?' And then he starts to feel really sick, he can barely breathe and the flies just keep appearing. They're all up in his grill and then the door suddenly creaks open and a terrifying, demonic voice orders him to '*Geeeeett ooouuuuut!*'? Try to do it like that and Jurgen will soon get the message and fuck right off.

# The Night I Pleaded With The IRA to Put Their Arms Away

June 2001. I am still drunk from the very liquor of my own tactical majesty, after leading Bolton Wanderers back to the Premier League a month earlier with a thumping 3-0 victory over David Moyes' Preston North End in the first division play-off final at Wembley. It was a triumph that dragged the unique splendour of my devastating innovation into the spotlight like never before. A performance so good that the great Barry Fry described it as 'the finest exhibition of football that I have ever seen'.

As preparations for our first season back in the Premier League began in earnest, I sat down with the Bolton board to discuss my plans. 'What do you want, big man?' they asked.

'I want Bruno N'Gotty from Marseille – a loan deal is fine – and Henrik Pedersen from Silkeborg IF,' I replied. 'Get me these lads in and watch me tear up this so-called top division like a quivering fanny.'

The board agreed instantly. I was the hottest managerial talent in the game that summer, and they knew they had to keep me sweet. As they began to wrap up the meeting, I leaned back in my chair. I wasn't done yet. 'I want one more thing,' I said. 'I want a few days off so I can go to Belfast and talk to the IRA about decommissioning their arms.'

Silence swarmed over the room like middle-aged women on a *Minions* meme. Eventually some anonymous, chinless executive piped up.

'Pardon?' he said.

'You heard me. Do you not watch the news, Poindexter? The short bits at the end? The peace process there is on the brink of collapse. I've sat and done nothing as countless peace accords in the Middle East have crumbled, and I refuse to let it happen again. I want to go to Ulster and sort this shit out once and for all.'

After a few more minutes of awkward silence, and several furtive glances amongst themselves, the board agreed to my request – on the condition that I took my then-assistant Phil Brown with me.

'He's a firecracker,' said one board member. 'It's like fucking *Mad Max* over there. You'll need all the muscle you can bring.'

Before Phil and I made the trip, however, we knew we needed someone to help us bone up on a bit of Irish history, not to mention hook us up with a connection in Belfast. Luckily, we knew just the man. Gareth Farrelly was a trusted member of my Bolton squad at the time and actually scored the first goal in the win over Preston. Gareth and I ended up having a bit of a falling out but I've always thought he was a good egg. I recently read that he's now a trainee solicitor. Being a trainee anything when you're in your 40s is embarrassing, quite frankly, but it does show what a smart head he has on his shoulders. Crucially for us, he was also Irish.

Phil and I pulled Gareth into the office and, after a bit of general chit-chat about The Troubles, we briefed him on the situation. 'Is this a joke?' he said, bewilderment etched all over his charmingly gormless face. 'Is this for Comic Relief or something?' Phil and I glared back at him with contempt. We would never support Comic Relief. 'The IRA? The real IRA?' he continued.

'No, the Provisionals,' I said, correcting him.

'No, I don't mean ... I just meant ... actual IRA men?'

'Yeah, but you said Real IRA. They're different aren't they?'

'More radical,' said Phil.

'Look,' I said, my voice rising in frustration as the conversation began to digress. 'Phil and I are going to Belfast tomorrow, we want to meet with the IRA and tell them to pull their fingers out and ditch those bloody guns. Can you help?'

Gareth's expression remained one of complete and utter befuddlement. 'Boss, why would I be able to help you meet with the IRA?' he asked.

'You're Irish, aren't you?' I replied.

'We don't all know lads that are in the IRA, chief.'

At this stage Phil had had enough. He leapt to his feet and pushed over the table. 'Tell us!' he screamed. 'Tell us now or I'll eat your pikey fucking balls! I'll eat both your balls and your filthy little cock!'

Gareth was speechless. I mean, Phil dutifully played bad cop to my good cop with the players in training often enough – the DCI Burnside to my Sgt June Ackland, if you will – but this was an escalation.

I sat back and smugly waited for the inevitable crack to snake down Gareth's bullish facade, but somehow it never came. He maintained his insistence that he didn't know anyone in Belfast, never mind in the IRA. Eventually, I lost my patience, made a really rather dreadful comment about Oliver Cromwell's role in Ireland, and told him to get the fuck out of my office.

In the end, we travelled to Belfast without a lead, and hoped for the best. We spent the first three days drinking and, as is so often the cause, alcohol provided the solution. On the third day on the lash, we got chatting to a local taxi driver called Brian in a seedy little pub in the city centre. As my tongue became ever more loosened by the libations, I decided to tell Brian about our quest.

'You football managers are all rich, aren't you?' asked Brian curiously.

'Yes, yes we are,' I replied with a smirk, before burning a ten-pound note and laughing my head off.

Brian folded his arms and smiled. 'I reckon I can help hook you up with the people you seek. One question, though. Why is he wearing a karate uniform?'

We both looked at Phil, who smiled back obliviously. He had turned up to the airport wearing a full karate gi and had worn it every day since.

'I don't know, Brian,' I said, sadly.

The following evening we rented a car and drove it to the Republican stronghold of the Falls Road, in the west of the city. As per Brian's instructions, we parked in a dark, desolate street behind an abandoned warehouse. There, we sat and waited to meet two men who, according to Brian, were 'absolute top brass members of the movement'.

As we sat in darkness, Phil put up his hand.

'Yes, Phil,' I said. 'You have a question?'

'Yes, boss. Why are we here again? Are we joining the IRA?'

I ruffled his hair with a chuckle, and plucked a stray hair off the lapel on his karate gi. He was fucking adorable at times.

'No, son. We're just here to talk. See if can we convince them to get rid of their guns.'

'Do they not want to?' asked Phil.

'Good question, Philip. They were supposed to have done it already, but there's no sign. And things are getting pretty damn tense around these parts as a result.'

Phil put up his hand again.

'Yes, Phil?

'Kevin Nolan says IRA is short for 'I rim arseholes'. Is it?'

'Be quiet now, Phil. There's a good lad.'

Before Phil had the chance to defy me and open his inane fucking mouth again, a car turned slowly into the street ahead. It stopped in the middle of the road, and, after a few excruciating seconds, the driver flashed his lights. This was our signal. Phil and I looked at each other.

'Here we go, champ,' I said. 'Are you ready?'

'Am I going to have to let someone tongue my bumhole, Dad?'

'For fuck's sake, Phil, stop going on about arseholes. Let's just go. Leave the talking to me.'

We exited and walked towards the other car, which had now parked up. The walk couldn't have been more than 50 yards but it felt like 50 miles. As we got closer, the driver turned off the headlights. I could see for the first time that the car was a BMW 5 series with blacked-out windows. As I peered through the windshield, trying in vain to get a look at the potentially deadly passengers that were sitting inside, the severity of the situation suddenly slammed into the back of my head with an almighty thump. I couldn't back out now, though. I had to go through with it. I took one last look at Phil, who was standing at the opposite rear door. I could tell from his expression that he was still worrying about analingus, the daft prick, but I took one deep breath and gave him the nod. We entered the car.

The driver and passenger continued to look straight ahead. From what I could see, they were fairly nondescript-looking. Both wore black jackets and hid behind thick, fake beards. Clever. Very clever. After a few seconds of studying us through the rear-view mirror, the driver spoke.

'My name is Paddy and this here is Malachy.'

Malachy nodded. It was to be the only gesture he made throughout the meeting. He was the absolute spit of Brian, now that I think of it. Wonder if they were related.

'We are in the IRA,' said Paddy.

'Do you have any ID?' asked Phil.

I froze. Phil asked some stupid fucking questions at the best of times but this was an absolute banger. I fully expected Paddy to pull out a gun and shoot us both in the face. His cold, black eyes burned into Phil's like laser beams. 'Yes,' he said. 'Yes, we do. Not on us, though. We're getting our cards laminated. Aren't we, Malachy?'

Malachy nodded again. I breathed a sigh of relief. I was also quite impressed, truth be told. Laminated ID cards? I'm dead against the IRA, but that's a touch of class right there.

'Now ... talk,' Paddy ordered us dispassionately.

I composed myself and explained to Paddy why we had travelled to Belfast and why we desperately wanted to meet the IRA. I told him the fate of this land was in the balance and implored him and his organisation to do the right thing – decommission their arms and dedicate themselves to a new Northern Ireland, forged by the political will of both sides of the community.

He looked at me for what felt like an eternity, his lifeless eyes scaring my balls right out of their sack. He then motioned towards Phil.

'Why is he wearing a karate uniform?'

I needed a proper answer this time. Paddy looked suspicious and I had to act.

'He's retarded, Paddy. He's hugely retarded.'

I looked at Phil. His face was sadder than the first ten minutes of Pixar's *Up*.

'Am I, Dad?' he asked.

I didn't answer him. I was too busy watching Paddy's eyes in the rear-view mirror. Trying desperately to read him. He stroked his fake beard. 'Look, we want to get rid of these weapons, but it's a pain in the bloody arse. The whole thing costs an absolute bomb, pardon the pun, and we just don't have the money.' Paddy shook his head ruefully and rolled his eyes. Such naked honesty from an Irish paramilitary. What a truly momentous occasion I was bearing witness to. I felt like fucking Attenborough.

Paddy went on to explain the logistical difficulties of decommissioning; hiring trucks to transport the guns to the desert, buying industrial-strength cauldrons to melt the guns, finding a big enough well to pour the melted gun metal down into. It *did* sound like a fucking nightmare. The delay in decommissioning, it transpired, was due to a simple lack of funding. The IRA was desperately looking for donors, but it was proving pretty difficult. What ruddy idiot wants to give money to the IRA?

This ruddy idiot, that's who. I told Paddy that I had heard enough and that we would be proud to be able to make a contribution to this historic moment in Irish history. I asked him to take us to the nearest ATM, where we withdrew as much as we could and presented it to the two men.

'Take this as a token,' I said dramatically. 'A symbol of our friendship, and a small donation towards a new Ireland. A new Ireland that can look to the future, with the support of the people of Great Britain.'

I then launched into a very moving rendition of 'Sunshine on Leith' by The Proclaimers. Halfway through the song, I remembered that The Proclaimers were actually Scottish, but it didn't matter. I looked at Paddy and Malachy. They were speechless. I'd touched them on a very deep, spiritual level. These men of violence sat motionless as their hearts were melted by the actions of a simple football manager from Dudley.

Paddy drove us back to our car. I asked him humbly if our contribution would make a significant difference to the whole process. 'Oh, aye,' said Paddy with a glint in his eye. 'Fucking massive, pal.'

As they drove off, I could hear them both laughing hysterically. It was the sound of pure joy. Relief as well, probably. Just think how hard it must have been for two hardened Republican men from Belfast to meet up with a couple of strangers and take money from them. To accept an olive branch from the old enemy across the Irish Sea. I couldn't help but be impressed.

In August 2001 – two months after I secretly met with them – the IRA unequivocally agreed to destroy its weapons. It was an historic, deeply significant moment in Northern Ireland's attempts to move forward as a truly peaceful society. Just how vital were the talks I chaired in that lonely backstreet in Belfast? How valuable was the £4,600 and the £40 that myself and Phil contributed to the process respectively? I guess we'll never know but, 16 years on, as I look at the vibrant, peaceful paradise that Northern Ireland has become, I can't help but swell with pride. I've since tried to keep an eye on what's going on across the Irish Sea and, while I'm never one to blow my own trumpet, I know that each child that is born into a prosperous and peaceful Northern Ireland, is able to do so because of me. It ain't a bad feeling, guys. It ain't a bad feeling.

# Six Dead Celebrities I Have Slept With

When I agreed to write this book, I was keen to establish just what exactly the publishers wanted from it and so I used a trick I often use on my players; I challenged them to sum up exactly what they wanted to achieve in three words. 'Provocative, salacious and *real*' is what they came back with. Probably paid an agency about £20,000 to come up with it as well. Pricks.

I sat down with a cool bottle of raspberry Yop and contemplated their vision. Provocative and real? Please. I'm as provocative as a handsome Nazi in just about everything I do, while the bandana I'm wearing as I type this was signed by the singer from the Bloodhound Gang, so you better know how real I am, son. But salacious? This concerned me a little.

I'm a sensual man, and one who is more than willing to divulge his own sexual practices and preferences for money. Talking about the many women I've laid down with, however, is another matter altogether. Especially when said women are also in the public eye.

That's what publishers want, right? They're not interested in the time I fingered plain ol' Helen Slattery in a skip outside Wembley while the new stadium was being constructed, or when I got a rusty trombone off some tart called Wanda on the dancefloor at the LMA awards dinner, while my peers stood around me applauding. No, they only want to hear about which member of Alisha's Attic I dry-humped at the Brits, or what Rantzen did to me backstage at *Children in Need* to make me scream like the start of 'Gett Off' by Prince.

I angrily rejected the sordid demands of the publishers, reminding them that, in contrast to their sleazy world, my dignity, and the dignity of the famous women that I have loved over the years, is not something that is for sale. Then they pointed out that you can't defame a dead person, and asked if I had any tales about boning famous, deceased broads that I'd fancy writing about, and I said, 'Yeah, no bother.'

Below, in no particular order, are six of the most sensational celebrity lovers that I've ever had. Who are now dead. Their bodies are buried in peace, but their name liveth forevermore. They may all have been one-night stands, but to quote Sarah Connor in *The Terminator*, in the few hours we had together, we loved a lifetime's worth.

## Margaret Thatcher

The Iron Lady, with the minge of silk. I'm not particularly proud of this one but it happened and it was sensational. I loathed everything about Margaret Thatcher. Everything except her rapacious appetite for porking. I met her in 1985 at one of Bruno Brookes' legendary midnight sex parties. She looked over at me as she sat at the bar, being bored shitless by Paul Young. As an oblivious Young yammered on, Thatcher rolled her eyes dramatically at me and grinned. I didn't smile back. The very sight of her made me sick, quite frankly. Her cruel politics were the very antithesis of what I stood for and her hair was fucking appalling.

I tried to carry on with my night, but Thatcher was watching my every move. She soon cornered me by the buffet, as I tried to have it off with a very drunk Sue Pollard. 'Hi-de-hi!' purred Thatcher satirically, as she slid up to me like a snake. Pollard was too out of it to even hear the reference. I simply ignored it and continued to chop up some French stick without so much as an acknowledgement of what the prime minister had just said.

'That's a big baguette,' she continued, coquettishly. 'Have you got any for me?'

This time, I did look at her. My resolve was starting to weaken: cuisine-based double entendres have always sent blood to my dong quicker than a slag jumping into a limo. Despite my now throbbing libido, I reminded myself just what this woman was capable of, and redoubled my efforts to stand firm. I flashed her a look of pure contempt. 'The way you smashed those trade unions was bloody sickening, you vampiric ghoul,' I spat.

'You can smash my trade union,' she retorted, clumsily. Pollard was on the ground by now.

This lascivious tête-à-tête went on for six more minutes with my willpower ebbing away all the while. Eventually, though, Thatcher grew impatient, and that infamous temper began to rear its ugly head. 'Listen, Pork Chop,' she said brusquely, 'I have a country to ruin. I can't stand here talking dirty all night. Do you want to loaf it into me or what?'

In spite of the protestations emanating from every last moral fibre in my body, the answer, sadly, was 'Yes,' and soon I was making love with Margaret Thatcher in a cubbyhole under the stairs at Bruno Brookes' house. We had intercourse three times in quick succession and it was hard and intense and vaginal. I did ask her if I could do her up the Bisto-chute as well, but she was having none of it. She shook her head wryly and whispered, 'The lady's not for turning.' Then she kissed me lightly on the forehead and left the cubbyhole that we had just made our own.

A few minutes later she left the party. I watched from the window as she got into Norman Tebbit's side-car and zoomed off into the night. Tebbit had sat waiting outside on his bike for the entire evening. The fucking bell-end.

I never voted for Thatcher before our tryst, and I certainly didn't vote for her after. Despite everything else, I'm still incredibly proud of that.

## The mum from *The Golden Girls*

I have to hold my hands up here and admit that I still don't know what her real name was. Blanche something? No matter what she was called, she was a tender lover, and a very sweet dame who oozed class. I banged her in a restroom at the premiere of *Stop! Or My Mom Will Shoot*.

I didn't care much for the movie, but I loved her performance. She portrayed Sylvester Stallone's meddling mother in it, and, while it was mostly played for cheesy laughs, the film did raise some really interesting questions about just how much involvement a parent should have in the life of a clearly retarded child. I don't think the movie ever got the credit it truly deserved for asking these questions, either. A real shame.

Stallone may have got top billing, but there was absolutely no doubt who the real star of the show was. That may be my unabashed bias seeping through, though. I absolutely adored her in *The Golden Girls*, and I've still got every episode of its lesser-known spin-off, *The Golden Palace*, on tape. I am an unrepentant fan-boy of ... whatever her name was, and when I saw her in the flesh at the premiere of *Stop! Or My Mom Will Shoot*, trying to slip quietly into a bathroom during the interval, I couldn't help myself. I knew it was the perfect opportunity to say 'Hello', and maybe get her autograph. It was perhaps the only opportunity I would ever have. I took a deep breath, and sidled up to her like a silent, ninja nonce.

'Going to shit out some cheesecake, maw?' I quipped. She looked momentarily startled, before a big grin broke out on her pleasant, craggy face.

'Funny,' she said, with a smile.

'Let me sit beside you for the rest of the movie and I'll make you laugh like a drain all night,' I said. A little trite, perhaps, but I saw an open goal and I went for it. I really wasn't sure where the ball was going, though.

'Aren't you a pushy little thing?' she said flirtatiously. Back of the fucking net.

'You don't usually smile on TV,' I said. 'You're usually dead grumpy. You should smile more. It's attractive.'

Her smile widened. I bet her wispy old fanny did as well, after a cracker of a line like that. 'Do you want me to sign that, sweetie?' she asked, pointing at my autograph book. I nodded my head. 'That's no problem,' she continued, 'but why don't you come into the restroom with me and I'll do it in there? That way we can have some privacy. Plus, I'm actually touching cloth here, honey.'

The next few minutes were amongst the most bizarre of my life, as I stood by the sink in a restroom in a Beverly Hills movie theatre, watching the mum from *The Golden Girls* take a shit.

'What do you do?' she asked. It was quite touching that this Emmy- and Golden Globe-winning television icon was taking an interest in a then-ordinary man from Dudley, but I knew full well that she probably just wanted to keep talking to mask the sounds of the plops below.

'I'm a football coach from England,' I answered. 'I'm going to be the best football coach England has ever seen.'

'You bet your boots you are, sweetie!' she said, kindly. She mistimed her sentence this time, however, and proceeded to produce the loudest plop that I have ever heard. It sounded like someone throwing a tyre into a canal. She locked eyes with me, embarrassment etched all over her face. 'These dumb movie premieres always make me tense,' she said coyly.

I didn't reply. I couldn't. By now, the stench was really starting to upset me. 'I might wait outside,' I stuttered, trying not to breathe in any more of her wicked crud. Before I could make a move, though, she jumped off the potty and threw her arms around me. 'I don't normally do this, but you're all sorts of cute, mister. Kiss me.'

I kissed her passionately. She had such soft lips for a 69-year-old. She suddenly broke away and, without breaking eye contact, checked that the door was locked.

'I've to get back to the theatre in a few minutes,' she said. 'Do you want to upgrade this kiss to something more ... meaningful?'

'Do you want to wipe your arse first?' I answered.

Evidently, she didn't. Instead, she sat back down on the toilet, pulled me towards her and began to make love to me. The sex was sweet. *Real* sweet. I soon forgot all about her unwiped hoop.

'Is this real, or am I dreaming?' I shrieked giddily. 'Pinch me, maw!'

'I can't, pumpkin, I'm already pinching this loaf,' she replied, crudely.

That's right. Despite the passion, and sheer intensity of the situation, she actually continued to take a dump as we copulated. Honestly, it was just plop after fucking plop. Each thrust I made seemed to be accompanied by another load falling into the bowl. It must have been stacked up like a fucking termite mound. To this day, I still don't know how such a tiny woman could produce so much waste.

Once we had finished, she dusted herself down, wished me well in 'the soccer' and left without flushing. Despite poor reviews, *Stop! Or My Mom Will Shoot* was reasonably successful at the box office, bringing in a total of $70.6 million worldwide.

## Whitney Houston

Due to the utmost respect I have for her family, and my absolute fear of reprisals from Bobby Brown, I shan't confirm where or when I got it together with Whitney Houston. In fact, I won't give any details at all.

All I will say is … you know when you're at a urinal, and you hold the end of your tadger so the piss builds up and your shaft ends up looking like a massive water balloon and then you let go of it suddenly and all the piss flows out like a tremendous waterfall? Whitney liked me to do something similar to that at the end of sex. It was fucking sensational.

RIP, my songbird.


## Chyna

If you have even a cursory interest in me and my life-style, you'll know that one of my true loves is the world of professional wrestling. While I was certainly fond of the corny, home-grown brand of wrestling that appeared on *World of Sport* when I was a lad, it was the glitzy, beefcake universe of the World Wrestling Federation – later renamed WWE after some panda-bothering cunts got too big for their hemp-fucking-boots – that truly gripped me and made me fall in love with the sport.

I've had some of the greatest nights of my life watching the superstars of the WWE grapple, including a trip to New York City to attend SummerSlam 91 with Woody Allen and Soon-Yi.

Back then, Soon-Yi was still Woody's … daughter, I guess? Or his wife's daughter? Is that right? I really don't know. All I do know is that Woody kept winking at me and whispering, 'When in Rome, eh?' with a rather unsavoury cackle. The whole thing was murky in 1991 and it's still murky now.

Despite all this, I had an absolute blast at Summer-Slam 91. Aside from all the totally awesome ringside action, one of the highlights of the evening was meeting the great 'Mean' Gene Okerlund. Mean Gene is, without question, the finest interviewer in the history of professional wrestling. He became a very close friend and over the years has helped me meet some of my greatest WWE heroes, including 'Ravishing' Rick Rude, The Honky Tonk Man and Tugboat. On a bitterly cold night in December 2001, in Chicago, Illinois, Mean Gene also introduced me to Chyna.

For those of you who don't know, Chyna was a former WWE women's champion and the only female to ever win the WWE Intercontinental title. Mean Gene knew I was a massive fan and so he kindly arranged for her to meet me for a drink. I still suspect he might have paid her to do it, but he has always been absolutely steadfast in his denials.

A truly extraordinary athlete, Chyna was often referred to in the WWE universe as the 'Ninth Wonder of the World' and, boy, they weren't wrong. She was 6 feet and about 13 stone of pure muscle, and when she walked into the hotel bar in downtown Chicago, I was awestruck and a little intimidated.

I was the manager of Bolton Wanderers at the time and, as we had a free weekend, I travelled to Chicago to watch a WWE show and catch up with Mean Gene. Some of the WWE superstars were also staying at the hotel, and as Chyna had recently left the company on less than agreeable terms, she was understandably a little uncomfortable.

Mean Gene explained to me that her relationship with WWE star Triple H had come to an end and he was now involved with Stephanie McMahon, the daughter of WWE owner Vince McMahon. 'Chyna suspects Triple H was seeing Stephanie long before he broke it off with her,' explained Mean Gene, 'so she's still a little bit raw.'

'Ker-fucking-ching,' I muttered to myself.

Gene introduced us and helped us break the ice with some classic small talk, before leaving us alone at the bar as he went to mingle with the other wrestlers. In contrast to her hulking frame, Chyna was very shy and softly-spoken. She was also clearly troubled. She seemed very nervous and was obviously still hurting from her break-up. She had also blacked herself up for some reason, which I thought was a bit weird.

'I really am a big fan,' I said, bashfully. 'I just ... I just love what you do.'

'You're very sweet,' she replied modestly. 'That means a lot.'

'You're sexy, too. Why did Triple H dump you?'

Chyna, unsurprisingly, began to bawl.

'Oh, shit, I'm sorry,' I backtracked. 'You're obviously still hurting. Why are you blacked up though?'

Her crying got even louder. She was starting to make a scene now. Chris Benoit began to give me dirty looks from the other side of the bar. Looking back now, he had some fucking nerve.

'Can't you see why I'm blacked up,' she blubbered. 'Isn't it obvious?'

'Not really, love,' I replied, bluntly.

'I've been betrayed and hurt by the people I trusted the most. I have been treated like a slave. Just like the millions of black people who have been enslaved for hundreds of years in this so-called United States of America. Now do you understand?'

I still didn't, to be honest. I thought her analogy skills were all over the fucking shop, truth be told, but I could see that she just needed a friend. I ordered two more Martinis and tried to lighten the mood. As usual, alcohol did the trick, and soon the conversation was much more ebullient. She regaled me with stories about the WWE, including some jaw-dropping tales of the backstage shenanigans. In return, I enchanted her with yarns about Bruno N'Gotty, who I had recently signed, and the size of his penis.

'Honestly, Chyna, it's like three Kit Kat Chunkys stuck together end-to-end,' I roared, as she doubled up with laughter.

We were getting on like a house on fire, when she began to look at her watch. 'I guess I better get a cab,' she said. 'I don't have a room here at the hotel.'

My whip-smart brain pinged into action. 'Good thing I have one, then,' I retorted, playfully.

She giggled and began biting the straw in her drink. I knew right there and then that I wanted to make love to this magnificent creature. Unfortunately, I'd had about 14 Martinis by this stage and, as I've explained before, my comprehension skills really do take a pounding when I'm on the sauce, so this feeling manifested itself in a less-than-delicate manner.

'I want to sex, you fucking beast!' I shouted.

She stopped biting the straw and looked me dead in the eye. If this was a movie, this would have been the moment when everyone else in the room stopped in their tracks and stared in my direction, accompanied by the sound of a vinyl record scratching to a halt. I'm a big man, but I looked like Pee Wee-fucking-Herman next to Chyna, and I fully expected her to lift me high into the air and smash me through the bar for my disrespectful words. Instead, she began laughing hysterically.

'Well, then,' she purred, once she'd stopped guffawing. 'Let's go up to your room and see if you've got what it takes.'

Ker-fucking-ching.

When we got to the room, Chyna sat me down on the bed, and started laying down some ground rules.

'I don't mind some rough stuff, buddy, but if you pee on me or do anything too kinky, I'll snap you like a Butterfinger bar.'

I didn't know what a Butterfinger bar was, but I got the picture. I reassured her that I was a meat and potatoes kind of guy, and overly kinky stuff wasn't really my bag.

'Well, I'm not sure I believe that,' she giggled. 'What does a big, sexy dude like you like to do?'

'I like to sit naked on a leather sofa and slowly peel my ballbag off the seat,' I replied, earnestly.

'Fair enough,' said Chyna, after a rather uncomfortable few seconds of silence. She was undeterred, and ripped my clothes off me in one single swipe. 'Let the dog see the rabbit, then,' she muttered, before pouncing on me like a leopard.

We made love all night, covering as many of Chyna's favoured sexual positions as possible. Most of the positions seemed to have striking similarities to wrestling moves, but I didn't object. At one point we did a 69er, with Chyna holding me upright. She then forgot herself for a moment, and pile-drivered me into the floor. When I regained consciousness, she apologised, made me some lemon tea and then continued to sexually demolish me.

As the ordeal continued, I became ever more bashed-up. I'm a huge advocate for sex-based innovation, but this was rough stuff. She had one position that she had created herself called The Fuck You Steph, which just seemed to involve her punching me square in the face while she bounced up and down on my now-destroyed tadger. We finished with Chyna putting me in a camel clutch. Despite the fact that such a move calls for me to be on my stomach, face-down, with Chyna astride my back and pulling my chin upwards with her interlocking fingers, she was still able to maintain full penetration between us. How she got our respective junk to connect in that position is still utterly beyond me.

'Pain and pleasure!' she shouted as we rocked back in forth in sexual majesty. It seemed to be mostly fucking pain to me, but I gritted my teeth and just went with it. Despite the fact that she angrily referred to me as 'Triple H, the king of the rice planters' all the way through this most aggressive of sexual congress, I eventually arrived at the sweet, relief-coated door of orgasm.

My one night with Chyna left me a broken man. I had several damaged ribs and a scrotum so bruised and swollen it looked like I was sitting on a purple fucking Space Hopper. I saw her again the following day, as I met up with Mean Gene for a farewell cappuccino before I flew back to England. She didn't speak a word about the previous night's antics, but I guess that was just her way. As we parted ways, I asked her if we'd ever see her back in the glitzy world of World Wrestling Entertainment.

'Maybe one day, buster,' she said with a cheeky wink. 'Maybe one day.'

She never did return, though. She went through the lesser wrestling promotions, before ending up in porn, making a couple of videos with her then-boyfriend Sean Waltman, who wrestled under the names 1-2-3 Kid and X-Pac. I hope she's found peace now. She's probably up there grappling with the angels as we speak. Or throwing them around their cloudy bedrooms and boning them so hard that their puny little angel knobs break like twigs. Either way, thank you Chyna. Thank you.

## Cilla Black

It was on an empty Palladium stage after a rather lack-lustre Royal Variety Performance. I was off my face on shrooms, and all I can remember is Cilla squealing, 'That's a lorra, lorra cock!' as I went about my carnal business. Jimmy Tarbuck was watching from the rafters, like some sort of perverted Phantom of the Opera. It was good. I liked it.

## Miranda Hart

[redacted at the request of Blink Publishing as Ms Hart is very much alive]

# Losing
# Your
# Virginity

Losing your virginity is one of the most daunting, stress-inducing rituals a young man can go through. I can still remember when it happened to me, on a cool autumn evening in 1970.

I was a fresh-faced, 16-year-old rascal, with tight, pastel-coloured slacks, a long, flowing mane and a vibrant sense of adventure. Every Friday night my pals and I would flock to Rockin' Rodney's Roller Disco, the hottest nightspot for under-18s in Dudley, and that is where I met her.

Her name was Deidre Swan, although I only found that out a few months after I met her. She went to a girls' school near mine and was a few years older than me. It's true to say she wasn't conventionally beautiful. She looked a little bit like Jocky Wilson, the late, great darts champion. She had his build too. Short, stocky and powerful. Oh, and she didn't have a right arm. She had a prosthetic claw thing instead;

little pincers, like Tee Hee Johnson from *Live and Let Die*. It was a little disturbing, truth be told, but I was still rather impressed by the cutting-edge technology. Some people in Dudley didn't have television sets in 1970 and yet, here she was, walking around with metal pincers, like some sort of giant, fairground claw crane.

I saw her from across the room. She was tucking into a packet of Quavers, plunging her claw in like a jackhammer, yanking the crisps out and shoving them into her gob with furious abandon. She wore bright yellow, cuffed trousers with a sassy matching bodysuit. Again, she didn't look *conventionally* sexy – she was fucking poured into those poor slacks – but something about it just worked. I fell for her instantly. The glamour, the poise, the singular determination to finish those crisps in a world-record time. While my ability to corral and seduce the fairer sex has since become a thing of legend, I was still quite shy back then. Plucking up the courage to speak to a girl was often an arduous burden at 16, but not that night. I have no idea why, but there was a serenity about me on that evening in Rockin' Rodney's, a bravery. I made a beeline for her immediately after spotting her.

She was sat on the bench at the side of the room. I rolled over towards her as she finished her Quavers and threw the empty bag on the floor. Litter is something I take pretty seriously, but I was too smitten to care. She sucked me towards her like a tractor beam.

'You get a lovely lot of Quavers in a bag,' I said, swirling around on my red-white-and-blue vinyl roller skates like Fred-fucking-Astaire.

'What?' she asked flatly.

'It's in the adverts, innit? For Quavers. Saw you eating them.'

'Oh. Nah. You don't get enough. I'm still starving.'

She then sucked some cheesy Quaver dust off the little pincers on her claw, dead seductively. The sound of her teeth as they clattered off the metal nearly made me blow my beans there and then.

'You're not wearing any roller boots,' I said. 'Don't you wanna jive?' With that, I started to jive.

'No,' she replied.

'Fair enough,' I countered.

At that point, Deidre stood up, brushed herself down with her good hand and slowly looked me up and down. She grabbed me by the collar of my pale blue chambray shirt and pulled me close. So close that I could smell the cheese on her hot breath. It was so hot. By this point, my plonker was harder than a granite kitchen worktop.

'Tell you what, podgy,' she purred. 'Buy me a sausage supper from that van outside and I'll let you fuck me the way Ted Heath is going to fuck this country.'

Sexually active AND politically-minded, with a grudge against the Tories to boot? I began to fall in love. Before I could even answer, she grabbed one of my belt loops with her pincers and pulled me across the dance-floor. As she did, I looked over at my friends, who had been standing at the side of the room, surveying the whole thing. They watched in stunned silence as I glided across the floor, being pulled towards manhood by big Deidre and her mechanical appendage. Their stillness spoke volumes. They were jealous, and rightly so.

As we got outside, Deirdre let go of me and sprinted towards the burger van. By the time I caught up with her she was wheezing as she tried to place her order. 'A sausage supper and two tins of Fanta,' she barked. 'And whatever this lad is having.'

I didn't order anything. I couldn't. The thought of food made me sick. My stomach was in knots. I was both excited and absolutely terrified. I was no stranger to my own genitals, but dealing with another person's junk was something else entirely. I was masturbating at a tremendous rate that year and could control the rhythm of my orgasm to an incredible degree. A few months earlier I'd started burping the worm to the sounds of 'American Woman' by The Guess Who and, by now, I was able to time my fuck wand to explode at 2 minutes and 15 seconds, when the guitar solo came to a crashing end. I played my plonker with all the deftness and violence of Randy Bachman playing his axe. It was stunning. I was no fool, though. Experimenting with onanism in the confines of your own bedroom, as your mother lies drunk on a beanbag downstairs, is no preparation for having to pleasure an expectant vagina.

I watched as Deidre sat on a wall beside the burger van and wolfed down her sausage supper and two tins of Fanta in no time. It took her less than 2 minutes and 15 seconds, in fact. I wondered if this was ironic. I wasn't sure. As she wiped the ketchup off her face with her own sleeve, she looked at me. 'OK, then,' she said with a belch. 'Let's go and pop that little weasel into the mulberry bush.' I didn't quite understand and my facial expression obviously attested to that. 'Let's fuck, fat lad,' she confirmed. With that, she hooked onto my belt loop again and ushered me towards an old mattress that lay beside the bins at the back of Rockin' Rodney's.

'Is it clean?' I asked as we sat down on the mattress.

'Well, it's not spotless, but I give it a good sponging once in a while.'

'No, I mean the mattress.'

'Oh. Yeah, it's fine. Is this your first time?'

I was rumbled. I didn't know much about women at that stage, but I knew that being a virgin wasn't a turn-on. 'No,' I said, trying in vain to sound defiant. 'I mean, yes. I'm a virgin. I've done some fingering but that's about it.'

Deidre chuckled and gave me a kiss. She then held up her pincers. 'I don't get much fingering done with these,' she said with a chortle. 'I'd pull out my fucking lungs.' We had a good laugh about that, and I instantly felt more relaxed. Being a virgin was always something to be ashamed of when you reached a certain age but, as I lay down on an old mattress beside some bins at the back of the local roller disco – with a sensual woman by my side – I honestly couldn't have cared less.

Deirdre held me in her arm. She stroked my hair with her claw.

'How did you lose one of your arms?' I asked.

'In battle, son,' she replied mysteriously. 'In battle.' And with that, we were off. She kissed me seductively, before snapping my belt off with her claw like she was some sort of sci-fi baddie, and pulling down my pants.

'Well, what have we here?' she said, her eyes widening. 'Someone was first in line when the cock factory opened.'

I smiled bashfully. It was true though; I had a cock like a Coke can. Still do. She took it in her pincers and squeezed it into her lady garden. 'Pop it right in there,' she said, before pulling me on top of her. 'Now – off you go.'

I'd never felt anything like it. It was like part of my body was somewhere else. Somewhere among the stars. I felt safe and secure. Every inch of my body tingled.

I never wanted the moment to end. Then, 11 seconds later, it did.

'Aaand ... that's your lot,' said Deidre, as she pushed me off her again.

'Is it over?' I asked innocently. 'Did I ... did I finish?'

'I hope so,' said Deidre. 'Otherwise there's something rotten dribbling out of my arsehole.'

'And did you ... did *you* come?'

Deidre burst out laughing and a bit of sausage that had been lodged between two teeth at the back of her mouth came free and hit me square on the nose. 'No, son,' she said, wiping tears from her eyes, 'but that's OK. The night is young.' She stood up and fixed herself. She ruffled my hair and pulled me to my feet. 'You're not a virgin anymore, sunshine. How do you feel?'

I'm not too ashamed to admit that I started crying. I bowed my head.

'It doesn't feel real, to be honest,' I said. 'It feels like my entire life was building up to this moment. I go into the night as a man now. A man who has experienced the most intimate thing two humans can experience. A man who has never felt so good. It's like ... things will never be the same, you know?'

I lifted my head to look at her but she had already walked away. She was at the burger van ordering curry chips and a can of Tizer. As I walked past her, I stopped and whispered, 'I love you.' She didn't hear me, though.

I went back to my friends and revelled in my newfound status. I was a man now, and everybody knew it.

I never spoke to Deidre Swan again. Some people say she was recruited by the army, who wanted to harvest her mechanical claw and use it as a weapon. Some say she moved to Walsall. I guess we'll never know. I've been with countless women since, every single one of them more beautiful and elegant, but none have had more impact on me than an average girl called Deidre. A stocky, enchanting princess who took my innocence in the palm of her metal claw and made me a man.

Losing one's virginity is unique. No two experiences are the same. The only thing of importance is to wait until you're ready, and enjoy every second of it. It won't be the best sex of your life, but you'll rarely experience anything as life-altering as the day you make love for the very first time. I think of Deidre every time I see an old mattress in an alleyway, or any time I walk past some bins. She made me the man I am, and I'll always cherish the brief moment we had together. I love you, Deidre Swan.

# My
# Grooming
# Ritual

There's no two ways about it; I'm a good-looking man. Don't believe me? Fire up your personal computer or your WAP-enabled telephone. Done? Next, get on to one of the Google or Bing or Ask Jeeves internet explorers and search for some photographs of me. Got one in front of you? Sound. Look at it closely. The smooth textures of the forehead, the adorable dimples, the chiselled jowls. I'm a fucking hunk. I'm in my sixties, yet I look about 20 years younger; I'd pass for Rob Lowe's little brother, for fuck's sake.

Does this physical effulgence manifest itself? No. No, it does not.

I've got good genes – and I don't just mean the Wrangler 1947 limited editions that have become my trademark (this gag will work better on the audiobook version). My mother was a difficult woman, but she was also very beautiful. Her sculpted cheekbones and to-die-for hips were just two of the things that I have inherited from her. Or is it four? How many cheek-bones and hips does the human body have? I don't know. Another one for Ask Jeeves, perhaps.

Yes, my genes are strong, but that's not enough to keep looking this good as you reach your sixth decade on this earth. This level of anatomical excellence takes a fuckload of work. It takes dedication to get up at 10.30 am EVERY SINGLE DAY when every last urge you have is telling you to have a lie-in. But I do get up. Why? Because I want to look as good as I possibly can, and I know I have work to do to accomplish that on a daily basis.

I'm not a young man anymore. I know that. I can't rely on metabolism to keep me glowing. We live in an ageist society, and staying on top of the game *mentally* is only one half of the battle. The other half is not looking like a fucking Weetabix in a suit.

It's not just about creams and ointments either. Grooming is a state of mind, and I'd like to share with you my grooming secrets. It's not a chore, either; I fucking love it. I love to groom. I'd groom you and your whole bloody family right now if I could! So, below is a summary of my grooming ritual. Read it. Learn it. Live it.

**10.30 am**: Depending on my employment status, this is the time I wake up every day. If I'm out of work, I might be a little bit more extravagant and snooze on until noon. I prefer to rise to the sound of some relaxing music, so I've ditched the polyphonic ring tones and set my phone to play songs from Spotify to wake me up. Kevin Nolan showed me how to do it and, honestly, it's like a breath of fresh air. 'Arthur's Theme (Best That You Can Do)' by Christopher Cross and 'Rape Me' by Nirvana are my current jams.

**10.40 am**: Have a big piss. I don't know what happens to me during the night, but by the time I wake up, I need to urinate so badly my cock and balls look like a water balloon that has been trodden on by a stiletto. My morning piss can take up to 130 seconds, and afterwards I honestly feel like I've already accomplished something for the day.

**10.43 am**: I brush my teeth with an Oral-B Pro 500 rechargeable electric toothbrush and a schmear of Arm & Hammer Truly Radiant. I brush for at least five full minutes or until my gums start pissing with blood, whatever comes first. Please do not panic if you see a little bit of blood. It just means you're doing it properly. It's the same when you're wiping your hole after a shit. It's just the body's way of saying, 'Thanks for the main-tenance, m'lord.' Sometimes I'll also give my chompers a bit of a floss. When I do, I use Oral-B Satin Tape. If I don't have any of that lying around, I'll just use a pubic hair. Honestly, the wife's pubes are like fucking cheese wire. There's always clumps of them dotted around her side of the bed. She sheds like a fucking Bernese Mountain Dog.

**10.48 am**: Full disclosure; until relatively recently I remained firmly, and rather stubbornly, a bath man. Sunday night was bath night when I was growing up, and the ritual just stuck with me, even as I entered adulthood. The wife and I used to love a bath on Sunday evening, before settling in for the night with some crackers and jam and the latest episode of *Birds of a Feather*. Having a bath was so much more than just a vehicle for hygiene. It was part of a decades-long routine that evoked only the happiest of memories.

Then one night the wife took a shit in the bath and that was that.

I got in after her as normal and, as I was leaning back, considering a crafty tub wank, her stinking release floated past my head like some sort of horrible little submarine. I took it in my hand and stormed downstairs.

'Does this belong to you?' I roared.

'Yeah,' she replied nonchalantly. 'I was wondering where that got to.' And then she laughed her head off. Twat.

As a result, I am now fully in the shower camp. I use Lynx Fever shower gel. The exotic scents, combining Brazilian hot mud and red dragon fruit extract, are utterly gorgeous and I just *love* the way it makes my bell-end feel all tingly. Some people gush about using face scrubs in the shower, but a good bar of soap is enough for me. One time at a hotel the wife couldn't find any soap. I eventually discovered a bar of Dove Original Beauty Cream tucked away at the back of the little cupboard under the sink. 'Look, love,' I said playfully. 'I found Dove in a soapless place.' Christ, we laughed.

**10.59 am**: It may be considered something of an outdated practice, but I still like to talc myself after a shower. First, I stand in front of the mirror and, with one hand, lift my scrotum towards my belly button. Honestly, don't be afraid of yanking that ugly little beanbag as hard as you can. It ain't coming off. With my free hand, I'll then go about applying the powder to my balls. I'll apply it good and proper, using about half a bottle of 300 g Imperial Leather Talc Original – maybe even more in the summer months. Sometimes talcing the lads will get me all hot and bothered. When that happens, a wank is inevitable. I just get it over with, have another shower, and start this phase all over again.

Once I'm finished on my cock and balls, I'll use the other half of the Imperial Leather on the rest of my body. Phil Collins once gave me a massive industrial-sized fan that was used on the video for Genesis' sublime 1991 cut 'I Can't Dance'. Sometimes I'll get the wife to pour the talc into the fan so it flies on to my body with dramatic intensity, but mostly I don't. It's really unnecessary.

Talcing up makes me feel fresh and confident. Some people have linked talcum powder to cancer, but I haven't.

**11.14 am**: Many people are repulsed by feet. Not me. If I had five minutes in bed with Kylie Minogue, I wouldn't go anywhere near her legendary rump. I'd spend every last second sucking on those adorable little toes. I, too, have beautiful feet. To keep them looking fly, I take a pumice stone to my tootsies each morning, getting rid of any dead skin, before slapping on liberal amounts of moisturiser. Doing this each morning might seem unnecessarily arduous in the winter months, but you'll reap the rewards come summertime, when you kick off your flip-flips at the beach and hear the awed gasps of reverence as everyone clocks your impossibly soft hooves.

**11.19 am**: Depending on the time of the year, I may need to trim my public thatch. A simple pair of household scissors suffices. It is important, however, not to cut off too much. I once went at it with a little too much vigour and made a hash of the whole thing. It looked like I had been in a fucking house fire; mismatched clumps of hair dotted amongst red-raw patches of skin. It was awful. It looked like Simon Weston down there.

**11.21 am**: I like my face to look as smooth as a baby's arse, so I shave every single morning without fail. I use the classic Bic 1 Sensitive disposal razor. Replete with iconic orange handle and fixed head, it utilises specially designed blade geometry for a smooth and close shave. You can also get a pack of 10 for about £2, so Bob's your uncle.

There are a whole host of foams and gels to choose from these days, so much so that it can be a little overwhelming. Should you go for Gillette? Or Nivea? Or King of Shaves? Should you get one with tea-tree oil? One that hydrates and moisturises your skin as well? Fuck that, I say. I go for Tesco's Everyday Value shaving foam. It's 50p per 250 ml, for Christ sake. My grandfather had to shave with a bayonet and a handful of petrol, so count yourself lucky and stop acting like a fruit.

**11.27 am**: Time to apply some aftershave. I've been using Brut by Fabergé since I was a teenager, and I'm sure as heck not going to stop now. It is the essence of man. Another fella smells that unmistakable scent off you and he knows he better not tangle with this rattle-snake. A lady gets one whiff of it and she knows she's in luck. She's in the presence of a real man. A swordsman that, if she plays her cards right, can make her wetter than Jeff Buckley's boots.

**11.29 am**: The pièce de résistance – the hair. Richard Keys once ran his fingers through my coiffure in the Sky Sports studios and said, 'This is how I think every muff should be. Feminism is a racket.' His issues with women notwithstanding, he was right about my hair. It's always been my pride and joy; thick, lustrous, magnificent. Now, while I'm all for eschewing unnec-essary expense with shaving foams and razors, I refuse to do the same with hair care. Only the best product is permitted to make contact with my glorious mane. My hair product of choice is Dax wax. The wave & groom range, to be precise. I carefully apply about a pound/pound and a half, and I sculpt for at least 15 minutes. Any less and I'm doing my hair a disservice, quite frankly.

I find that wearing heated Marigold kitchen gloves and using only the tips of your fingers is perfect for creating the short, edgy look that I have become known for. A layer of hairspray adds the perfect finishing touch. I opt for four short bursts, each lasting about three seconds, and I use whatever the wife has laying around. If your better half doesn't have any, a dollop of Crisp 'n Dry will do the trick.

**11.44 am**: It's the 21st century, folks. It's not just women and the gays that need to think about their skin. Take Sir Alex Ferguson, for example. That man is my hero. I love him like a father, but have you ever seen him close up? He looks like a McVitie's Ginger Nut. I ain't going out like that, so I use Nivea's Rehydrating Moisturiser. It immediately alleviates skin dryness and tightness while providing long-lasting moisture and care for the skin. I got it as a Christmas present from Barry Venison two years ago and, despite having a build-up of scum around the tip of the tube, it's still going strong.

**11.48 am**: The last and possibly most important part of my morning ritual. This one doesn't involve any sort of cream or lotion. It's not designed to exfoliate your skin or trim your cuticles. For this part, I simply stand in front of the mirror, naked and glowing, and chant, 'Today you will be the winner' over and over. Each time I chant, I get louder until, finally, I am screaming it at the top of my voice. Only then do I know that I am absolutely ready to take on the day ahead. Only then do I feel at my most beautiful.

# A Writer Writes

've been an apex football manager for a quarter of a century now and, it's safe to say, like many of my peers, I have become absolutely consumed by the game. I eat, live and breathe football. While this obsession has helped sharpen my abilities to an almost unbearably taut degree, it has taken its toll on other aspects of my life. I find it very difficult to relax, and almost all other hobbies that require a reasonable amount of dedicated time have fallen by the wayside. Stargazing, cobbling, breeding kestrels. These are just a few of my beloved pastimes that have slowly been absorbed and replaced by the increasingly insular dedication to my craft.

One thing that has endured, however, is my love of writing. I've written prose since I was a teenager and, while I don't pretend to be a Dickens, a Hemingway or even an Archer, it's something that I adore. After being sacked by Blackburn Rovers in 2010, I threw myself into my writing with ferocious vigour. The wife would often be woken by the sound of my quill scratching furiously against the papyrus as I hunched over the desk in my study, working by candlelight.

'What you doing up at this time, love?' she'd ask.

'Working on my latest piece, a mystery novel set in the olden times called *What Doth The Fog Bring?*' I retorted, barely looking up from my manuscript.

'Fair enough,' she said supportively.

As I got back into work, however, I found myself with less and less time to dedicate to writing. *What Doth The Fog Bring?* never got finished and my quill ran dry. It remained dormant for several years, until I took the job at Crystal Palace and teamed up once again with Sammy Lee.

Sammy is a great friend with an extraordinarily perceptive way about him. During a break in training one day, he popped into my office and saw me poring over a copy of L. Ron Hubbard's *Battlefield Earth*, making notes in the margins. I slammed the book shut when I noticed him at the door and asked what he wanted.

'What do *you* want, chief?' he asked with a knowing smile. 'That's the question.'

'I'd love a blueberry muffin,' I retorted, my devastating ability to quickly and deftly change the subject springing into action.

'A writer writes, boss man,' said Sammy with a chuckle. 'Don't walk the walk if you can't talk the talk.'

I was a little embarrassed by him catching me in the act and I didn't really like his tone, so I called him a 'little Fanta-pubed goblin', and told him to go and put the cones out. Deep down, though, I knew he was right. Referring to oneself as a writer has an air of romance about it, whether you're a successful, published novelist or someone that does it merely as a hobby; a release that keeps the creative juices flowing alongside the unwavering tides of everyday toil. It's easy to *call* yourself a writer, but it don't mean shit if you aren't *doing* it.

With that in mind, I began to write again. Any time I felt the stresses of the job get to me, I would simply lift up my quill. It barely left my hand after my first training session, when I was forced to watch Christian Benteke stumble around with all the grace of a fucking panda, but that was fine. It became therapeutic. I tried my hand at everything, from poems to essays, reviews to screenplays. I soon realised, however, that I had a particular adroitness for crafting short stories. I've written 93 of them in the last year alone. Most of them are just for me. A way for me to express myself. Perhaps, a way to *find* myself.

Being published has never been a goal. The idea of writing something that I am truly proud of, but never allowing it to be exposed to another pair of human eyes, is strangely thrilling. Like some sort of deeply personal respite from football.

After leaving Crystal Palace, however, I have been squirrelling away on one particular story that is a little different. A spooky little tale, I believe it marks a clear point in my development as a writer, and it's one, if you forgive my indulgence, that I'd like to share with you here in this book. Offered without comment and without a demand for acceptance, I give you ...

# The Night
# of The
# Stranger

It was little after 9 pm on a dark, windy night in November. Professor Crippin sat in his favourite chair in Harvard's Houghton Library. The library was the university's primary repository for rare books and manuscripts, so Crippin, a professor of English literature, was in his element there. He came here most nights to read. Aside from his work as a professor, he didn't have much in his life. His wife, Abigail, had died in mysterious circumstances a decade earlier, and he had few friends. He probably would have done himself in if it wasn't for those books. All those endless possibilities sprouting forth from each page. He read the Magna Carta one night in the library, front to back. Boy, he loved to read.

'All good, Prof?' said Steve, a hip young student who worked part-time at the library, as he sauntered past, carrying a big pile of books with him.

'Fine thanks, Steve,' replied the professor.

'You're the last person here tonight. What would we do without you and your love of the written form,' said Steve with a wink.

'Dunno,' said the professor with a chortle.

An hour passed without incident. There wasn't a sound in the library, save for the whipping of the winds outside and the sound of Professor Crippin turning the pages of his latest tome. He checked his watch. 'Probably time to go home,' he thought to himself. But to what? A silent, creaking house? The unrelenting white noise of the television? The guilt-inducing temptation to have a crafty wank in Abigail's old chair? None of those sounded appealing right now. He'd rather stay in the library and read, which he loved to do. Suddenly there was a bang in the north-eastern corner of the library. A loud, dull thud that he couldn't quite put his finger on.

'Steve?' he shouted. 'Did you fall or drop something? Is that what that bang was?'

No answer. He looked out of the window and into the car park. The only car there was his own; his beloved Acapulco-blue 1968 Ford Mustang Fastback Shelby GT500, a birthday gift from Abigail before she died. There was no sign of Steve's car either. It was also a Ford Mustang but nowhere near as nice.

What the fuck is going on? the professor wondered. Then ... BANG! It was another bang. It was even louder this time. 'Who's there?' stuttered the professor, who was really getting a dose of the willies now. All of a sudden the sound of a piercing scream rang out through the halls of the library, shaking the shelves and scaring the absolute shit out of Professor Crippin. It was like the start of *Ghostbusters*. The professor didn't want to hang around to see where the scream came from, so he picked up his belongings and ran for the front door. When he got there it was locked. From the outside. He looked helplessly out of the window. Then, like some sort of miracle, a pizza delivery boy cycled past. The professor banged on the window like a man possessed.

'Hey, kid!' he yelped. 'Hey, kid, help me! Open the door!'

Sadly, the delivery boy was Muslim. Or Hindu. Whichever one wears turbans, and the turban was pulled over his ears, so he couldn't hear. Agonisingly, he cycled past the library and out of sight. The professor wasn't a racist, but he really thought people from different cultures needed to assimilate better when they came to America, and this only served to confirm his view. The country was still in turmoil after President Trump had been murdered by Muslims, and the topic remained a real hot potato.

'Think, Nigel, think!' the professor thought to himself. His first name was Nigel. Then, he had a brainwave. The back door. There was a back door to the library. He could get out that way! Just one problem, though; it was in the north-eastern corner of the building. The exact place where the two thuds and the scream had come from. GODDAMIT!

Professor Crippin wasn't a brave man. He'd always known this of himself. A drunk, beefy man had once grabbed Abigail by the ass in a bar, and the professor did nothing. When she'd tried to tell him what happened, he just kept saying, 'What?' like he couldn't hear what she was saying, but he totally could. His cowardice that night had always shamed him. He wasn't going to make the same mistake twice. The professor took a deep breath and began to move towards the back of the library. As he did so he looked at some of his favourite books. A first edition of *Ulysses*, a rare hardback version of *The Catcher in the Rye*, the *Dead Sea Scrolls*. These books had been more than simply pastimes for the professor. They had become priceless companions in a life that had turned to absolute shite. As he passed them, he grew in confidence. These books weren't all going to come to life and help him like in that film *Night at the Museum*, but their very presence was enough to make him feel like he wasn't alone.

Professor Crippin reached the north-eastern corner of the library. As he did so, he heard a muffled cry. He turned the corner and his blood froze. There, in front of his very eyes, stood Abigail, his dead wife. She wore a pale pink dress, with her hair pulled back in a ponytail, just as she was wearing it the last time he saw her alive. She hadn't aged a day. A gorgeous orange glow snaked around her entire body, like in those old adverts for Ready Brek. She looked up and smiled.

'Abigail?' the professor said eventually, a single tear rolling down his cheek.

'Hello, Nigel,' she replied, her voice reverberating with an unworldly sound. 'How have you been?'

'I miss you, baby,' he said. 'What happened to you ten years ago? Your death was so mysterious.'

Abigail moved towards the professor. His instinct immediately told him to back away. It was his wife, but she was still a ghost. Then, a strange calm came over him. He walked forward until they were close to each other.

'I fell off that cliff near our house,' said Abigail.

'The Aquinnah cliffs in Martha's Vineyard, Massachusetts?' asked the professor.

'Yeah, them.'

Abigail's body had been found in a small stream some 30 miles from their house a decade ago. The police were never able to say what happened to her, but rumours of suicide and even murder had long persisted. The professor was glad to finally know the truth. 'What are you doing here?' he asked. 'I've missed you so much.' He reached out to touch her face, but his hand went straight through it like she wasn't there. Like she was a cloud or something.

'I'm afraid you can't touch me, my love,' she said with a smile. 'I'm a ghost. I know you come here every night and I just wanted to get in touch again and tell you to get on with your life. Go meet a woman, get on Tinder, anything but this library. You've your whole life ahead of you.'

'I have nothing but these books,' said the professor. Abigail was still the only person he could be honest with. 'I love to read,' he added.

'You should write one yourself,' said Abigail. 'You've read so many books, but I think you'd be a good writer. Try it. Remember … a writer writes. Don't talk the talk, if you can't walk the walk.' And with that, Abigail begin to float into the sky. As Nigel watched his wife leave him for a second time, he began to cry. Then he stopped crying and smiled. This was the beginning of the rest of his life. He'd do it. He'd write a book. He'd write a book for Abigail, his dead wife whose spirit was floating just yards above his head.

'What shall I call it?' he asked, as Abigail began to disappear into the ether.

'It depends what it's about, I suppose,' she replied. Then, just before she disappeared forever, she whispered something that remained with Professor Crippin for the rest of his life. 'You've become a stranger to life, my rose. Don't be a stranger, Nigel. Don't be a stranger.'

And with that, she was gone. Professor Crippin fell to the floor and began to sob. At that point, Steve, the lad who worked in the library, suddenly re-appeared.

'You all right, Prof? he asked. 'I popped out and got us a couple of coffees.'

The professor stood up. He wiped the tears from his eyes and smiled. 'You know what, Steve. I think I am all right. For the first time in a long while, I really think I'm going to be all right.'

'Wicked, professor!' said Steve with a smile. 'Wicked.'

A year later, Professor Nigel Crippin sat at a table in the largest branch of Barnes & Noble in New York City. His first novel, *The Night of the Stranger*, had sat proudly at the top of *The New York Times* bestseller list for the past three months. As a massive queue of fans waited to get their copies signed by the hottest new author in the literary world, the professor looked up to the sky and winked.

'You were right, baby,' he whispered softly. 'You were right.'

He laughed to himself for a moment, before pulling himself out of his short, pleasant reverie. 'Who's next?' he shouted, looking up to see the next eager face waiting in line for his autograph. As he did so, his blood froze.

There, at the front of the queue, in a pale pink dress and her hair pulled back in a ponytail, stood Abigail.

'Hello, Nigel,' she said, her voice firm and full of life. 'How have you been?'

The end

# Should Brexit Mean Brexit?

Yes. Yes it should.

# Six Ways to Keep Your Sex Life Vibrant

Few things are as invigorating as the thrill of a new relationship. The nervous excitement as you slowly open yourself up to someone new, the romantic way you agree with every single thing they say, the dreamy titillation of running your finger slowly up and down your perineum in the bath, as you wonder what their fanny is like. Love truly is a many-splendoured thing.

You know what they say, though? This thrill will not last. Sure, you can hope that this exciting new thing will evolve into a real and lasting relationship, but the butterflies you feel in those opening few weeks and months will soon fly away to be replaced by complacent, powdery moths. That unexplainable, ethereal electricity that permeates through your body at the merest glimpse of this person will soon disappear, leaving only a joint bank account, television box sets, and genitalia that you're sick of the fucking sight of.

Or will it ...

Keeping a marriage or long-term relationship fresh and exciting is difficult, but it is certainly not impossible. Time corrodes many things, but curiosity should never be one of them. If you can maintain a healthy level of passion, enthusiasm and wonder about your lover and the relationship you share, you can stay happy well into your later years, when mental illness and physical deterioration will obliterate everything that matters anyway.

I've been a happily married man for over 40 years. The road has often been rocky, not to mention fraught with pitfalls, but the wife and I have managed to retain a level of mystery and romance that has sustained us. While I know everything about her and have traversed every last inch of her body, the relationship can still surprise me. We work hard at keeping things fresh. It might be through a spontaneous bout of role play or a trusty, old-fashioned thumb up the arse, but we refuse to relent in our quest to keep the wolves of sexual mundanity at bay, and we reap the rewards.

Intercourse is the most important aspect of any romantic relationship. Once your sex life starts to suffer, the rest of your union will begin to crumble like cheap ham. Making love to your partner at least six times a week is absolutely essential, but in a world teeming with internet porn and erotic literature, the quality of the sex is just as important. A two-minute missionary job may have sufficed back in the 1970s, but not today. People want great sex. Intense, challenging, provocative sex.

Being able to fulfil these sexual needs is a tall order for most men, but I am here to help. My carnal capabilities are truly the stuff of legend. I once gave a woman the digitry for 53 consecutive minutes, enabling her to have 14 orgasms in a row. After she regained consciousness, she thanked me and said, 'I'd take your inquisitive fingers over a bag of big dicks any day of the fucking week.' You can't buy testimonials like that.

Below are six easy steps that will lead any man to a better, more fulfilling love life. Consider these pearls of wisdom the very building blocks of a rounder, more erotic lifestyle. Live by these rules and the roaring fires of lust will continue to burn for you and your partner well into your twilight years. Or until you meet someone nicer.

## Stay clean

Sex after you and your partner have just had a shower is wonderful thing. The smell of cleanliness can be the ultimate aphrodisiac, as you explore each other's immaculate, shimmering bodies. There's something almost spiritual about the experience. Your bodies feel brand-new. Every touch feels unique as you explore flesh that has just been born. You can have the confidence to stick your tongue pretty much anywhere.

Why not go one step further and make love *in* the shower? The feel of the water bouncing off your back, as you hammer one into your partner is almost mystical. Try it. You'll never look back.

If you do not have time to take a shower before intercourse, however, then at least run your cock under the tap for a couple of seconds. It could make all the difference.

## Get out of your comfort zone

For too many couples, sex is a drab, routine affair, played out in the same surroundings night after night. Why not take it out of the bed? Why not then take it out of the bedroom? Heck, why not go the whole hog, and take it out of the house entirely?!

Love-making in alien places can be hugely exciting. I don't mean alien places like Mars or fucking Jupiter. I'm a man of football, not science-fiction. I'm talking about getting out of your comfort zone. Having a romp in a place you wouldn't normally consider as conducive to sexiness can actually be quite a turn on. A bus stop, a skip or a beautiful, secluded countryside meadow can all be the perfect settings for getting your (thinking-outside-the-box) freak on.

However, if you want to take it a step further, how about environs that perhaps aren't so safely secluded? It might sound a little dangerous, but the fear of being caught can be such a rush. The wife and I once embarked on a 69er on the bonnet of a parked Volvo 440 on the Kings Road in London. I can't even begin to describe the thrill of it. An open-top bus full of American tourists stopped just as I was reaching my creamy crescendo.

'Gee, whizz!' shouted some fat hick, as he scrambled to take a photo of the erotic majesty he was witnessing.

'Gee-jizz, more like,' I screamed, as I spaffed my chowder everywhere. I don't think he heard me, though.

## Embrace role play

Familiarity breeds contempt, they say, and nothing can drain a relationship of its sparkle quicker than animosity. Put simply, you're far less likely to put in the hard yards in the bedroom when the mere sight of your partner makes you want to cry. This is where role playing comes in.

Why trudge on, having limp, monthly sex with Dorothy, your frumpy, soul-destroying wife of 18 years, when you can frolic erotically with Talulla-May, a husky-voiced pumpkin farmer from Alabama? Or LaQuanda, a black ... woman? Sex is about so much more than the insertion and thrusting of the penis, usually when erect, into the vagina for sexual pleasure, reproduction, or both. It's about the whole experience. The narrative. The setting. The *vibe*.

The wife and I are fully paid-up members of the role-playing club. Literally. Those two filth-mongers that own West Ham United also run a terrific – and, thankfully, invitation-only – online service for role-playing enthusiasts. For a monthly subscription, they'll post you out a beautiful little package with half-a-dozen role-playing options inside; costumes, props, narrative instructions – the lot. One particular package that I took delivery of a few months ago was an absolute corker, with the pick of the bunch being the Winnie the Pooh option. I dressed up like the aforementioned Pooh Bear while the missus transformed herself into a young Christopher Robin. It was utterly magical, managing to imbue us with an enchanting, child-like wonder that we so often lose when we reach adulthood, whilst still retaining a very adult, erotic edge. The sex was both exhilarating and innovative, the characters allowing me to open up sexually in a way I never have before. The props even included a dildo shaped like Eeyore. My honeypot took an absolute pounding, if you catch my filthy drift.

If talk about subscriptions and multi-layered role playing sounds a little too expensive and elaborate for you, then why not improvise with what you have? I once found an old LeBron James Miami Heat shirt in the back of my wardrobe, and decided to get creative. I used an old black tie as a makeshift headband, and painted my cock to look like a basketball. I ripped down the basketball hoop from the neighbour's back garden and placed it over the wife's bangle. I slam-dunked the absolute shit out of her all afternoon. All the way from downtown. It was fucking glorious.

The limits of your imagination really are the only boundaries when it comes to role play. It does have some downsides, though. You know when you finally climax during filthy sex and the lustful drive that was controlling your body mere seconds earlier just gets up and leaves and you immediately feel a sense of disgusting self-hate? Try looking into the mirror at that particular moment and seeing Winnie-the-fucking-Pooh leering back at you. It can really bring things home.

## Put on a show for her

The pressure to pleasure another human being during sexual intercourse isn't something to scoff at or take lightly. Worrying about your own performance is stressful enough, never mind having to consider how much enjoyment the other person is getting.

A very classy way to counter this is putting on a solo show for your woman. If you can turn her on without touching her, you're on to a winner. She'll be purring like a Cadillac by the time you do go in for the kill. While a simple lap dance, or a good, old-fashioned striptease, is perfectly acceptable, I have a slightly more bespoke routine to get my lady frothing at the muff. A typical solo performance from me might go something like this ...

I lie her down on a bed scattered with rose petals and begin to dance for her. Something high-energy and balletic. Erasure or Autechre, perhaps. I dim the lights, and fire up a few of my precious Yankee Candles – Autumn Night or Coastal Living. I'm wearing nothing but white stretch-cotton briefs and a silk robe. I take the soundtrack down a notch with 'I Swear' by All-4-One, or something by Sixpence None the Richer. One of the B-sides. I drape myself over my New Zealand sheepskin beanbag and begin to writhe in ecstasy, rubbing my chest and flicking my nipples. It's like a George Michael (RIP) video. The wife is moaning like a trapped pig. I've got her right where I want her. It's time for the main event.

What the missus doesn't know is that I've made a little hole in the groin of my cotton briefs. A hole just big enough to fit the tip of my thumb and index finger. I reach in and then slowly, but very surely, I begin to pull by ballbag through the hole. The wife is nearly in convulsions. She's whistling like a fucking kettle by now. She sounds like Serbian ultras booing a black lad. I continue to tease her, pulling my sack out inch by inch. The sensation is extraordinary, the tension almost unbearable. The wife is tingling with desire. I yank the reminder of my scrotum out of the hole in my pants, but I pull it with such force that the plonker comes out as well. All the lads are out in the open. The wife squeals orgasmically.

'Get that chubby little fuck wand over here right now!' she roars.

I leap off the beanbag like a cougar and onto the missus. The antipasto is finished; it's time for the main course. Of course, you don't need to be this elaborate. You can just let her watch you have a quick wank on the shitter if you prefer.

## Use food

I once got chatting to Edwina Currie at a rather rambunctious cocktail party for Michael Heseltine's 70th birthday. As we swigged on Sidecars, she leaned in close and told me how she had become a huge fan of using foodstuffs during love-making. Eggs, in particular.

It started as some sort of ironic comment on the 'salmonella in eggs' furore that she caused in Britain in the late 1980s, but soon she started to genuinely enjoy it, and the whole thing became post-ironic. She's such a fucking millennial. 'Hard-boiled, fried, scrambled or poached,' she whispered to me, her hot breath reeking of brandy. 'I don't care how it's prepared, big man; if I can get it in me or in him, then I'll fucking use it.'

As I've already mentioned, cleanliness is very important to me during sex, and so I'm very careful about what kind of food I introduce into my bedroom trysts. Spreading Nutella over your partner's bits and pieces may sound like a lot of fun, but cleaning it up afterwards is a different matter altogether. Have you ever had to deal with a congealed combination of hazelnut spread and semen? It's not nice at all.

I'd advise keeping things simple and bite-size. Keeping an erection flourishing as you tackle a fish supper is an impossible task. Whipped cream, syrup and fruit will – in small amounts – add a refreshing zing to proceedings, while a Mint Cornetto can escalate the tension no matter which end you use.

My confectionery of choice in the bedroom is, without question, the Curly Wurly. I adore having it slotted into my ringpiece, then being pulled out again slowly. If you strike the right balance, it can also make a lovely xylophone-like sound as it exits the anus. Please do be careful, though. Once a Curly Wurly was pushed in with too much vigour and the missus couldn't retrieve it again. It's probably still up there. I have no idea if it ever came out naturally. How would I?

## Try new positions

Fancy yourself as a bit of a swordsman? Reckon your own inner sex manual is crammed with all the carnal knowledge you could possible need? OK, then, hotshot – name as many sex positions as you can … Missionary, cowgirl, doggy-style … great – keep going. Oh, sorry? You're struggling? Thought so. Get back in your box, you cheeky fucking prick. You ain't no John Leslie, gringo.

There are literally hundreds of sex positions, and the average couple isn't even aware of the vast majority of them. Sure, you and Dorothy might go wild for a special occasion and opt for a reverse cowgirl, but that's mostly so you don't have to look at her fucking face and it isn't very adventurous at all. You're really just scratching the surface.

Don't be bashful about doing some research. Get onto your computer and Bing it. There are thousands of websites and publications that can teach you about every position known to man. Some of them even have little illustrations that can show you exactly how you can perfect them with your partner. Don't just limit yourself to the status quo though; try inventing some positions of your own. Experiment with your bodies. It doesn't matter how outlandish it might seem in your head, just give it a go. It doesn't matter how unholy you think the contortion may be, if your plonker can reach her doot, it's a sex position.

If you'll indulge me tooting my own horn for a moment, I've been hugely successful in transferring the innovation I am noted for on the football field to the bedroom. I've masterminded a number of devilishly inventive positions that the wife and I have been enjoying for years. The one that I am most proud of? Good question. I'd say it's probably The Chopper. It's a difficult one to master, and pretty hardcore, but if you can do it you'll be in sexual paradise. The missus lies on her back, holding her own ankles and pulling her legs towards her (that yoga voucher I got her on Groupon really has paid for itself ten times over). I then insert myself and, using my incredible physical strength, I balance myself on her, lie prone in mid-air and twirl my entire body like a helicopter rotor blade. Yes, I'm a bloody show-off, but it truly is an incredible spectacle to witness. More importantly, however, it feels extraordinary.

I should point out, however, that it is very, *very* important that you lube your tadger up good and proper for The Chopper. The penis needs to move in circles along with your body. If it stays firmly in place inside the vagina, it'll snap in half like a fucking ice pop the second the rest of your body starts pivoting. The fact the penis is rotating, rather than thrusting, leads to a really satisfying orgasm. The whole thing probably feels grand for the missus as well.

# How to
# Party Hard
# When You're
# Saddled
# With a
# Disabled For
# Company

That moment in a young person's life when he or she graduates from childish activities like hopscotch and stickball to socialising in more adult settings might seem a little trivial, but it is truly one of the most exciting transitions a person will make.

I can still remember standing at the back of Rockin' Rodney's Roller Disco with my friends in 1972. I was 17 years old, and the thrill of spending every Friday evening at an under-18's disco had long since worn off. My buddies and I were resigned to another evening of immature girls and brown lemonade when a member of the gang, Mark 'Walsho' Walsh, sauntered up to us with a smile on his face. 'Get your coats, boys,' said Walsho. 'We're going down the Tropical Sword.'

We look at each other in puzzlement. The Tropical Sword was a local nightclub and not somewhere we had ever been. We were no strangers to alcohol; we regularly got tanked up down by the quarry and there was one local pub that let us in – the owner had some sort of mental illness and, for some reason, seemed to think we were all estate agents in our 40s – but getting into a nightclub at 17 was a different matter altogether.

In spite of these reservations, young Walsho convinced us, and we all made our way to the Tropical Sword. It soon transpired that Walsho's older brother's friend was working the door that night and had promised to turn a blind eye if we wanted to gain entry. The sights and sounds that smacked me in the face as we walked into the place will live with me forever. The smell of smoke, hairspray and Cinzano wafted up my nostrils, as Michael Jackson's 'Rockin' Robin' blasted out from the speakers. Scores of burly, hirsute men danced erotically with lithe, voluptuous young women on the packed dancefloor. This was *real* dancing, too. Nothing like the kind of frigid child's play we were used to in Rockin' Rodney's. At the Tropical Sword, bodies became one. The music took over the physical form and flesh collided in glorious harmony. It was fucking brilliant.

We didn't participate much that night. We just stood at the side of the room, gawping at the action that unfolded around us. I don't even think we had a drink. Being part of that environment, even for just a few hours, was intoxicating enough. The whole thing was a real sensory overload for our young minds, and hard to take in. What was clear immediately, however, was the fact that there was absolutely no way we could go back to Rockin' Rodney's the following Friday night. There was only one place we wanted to be from now on, and that was the Tropical Sword.

Over the course of the next few years, we had some cracking nights out in the club. We laughed, we loved, we danced. We even smoked marijuana cigarettes when Chris Ellis's sister was there one night with her Nigerian boyfriend, Banjoko. It was a truly magical time. One thing, however, always threatened to place a little bit of a drag on proceedings, and his name was Alf 'Gooter' Daly.

Gooter was a nice lad. He was quiet, studious and terribly polite. He wasn't really part of our gang, but his older brother Greg was, and their mother encouraged him to include Gooter in anything we did. The Dalys were a big, loyal Irish family, and turning one's back on a sibling just wouldn't be tolerated. To Greg, Gooter was never a burden. It was a beautiful thing really, but it put some serious cramps on our style back then. Why? Because Gooter was a disabled.

I know what you're thinking. I'm a complete and utter bastard for even contemplating such a thing? I'm lower than a UKIP supporter with internet access? Try to remember, however, that I was just a young man at the time. Young men are often selfish by nature, with a hideously warped view of their own reputation. I liked Gooter, I really did, but in my vain, hormone-drenched mind, he was merely an unnecessary obstacle in my gang's attempts to look cool and attract women. Like all disabled people, he also wore terrible jeans. It all seemed like such a serious drain on our vibe.

Gooter had cerebral palsy. He was as bright as a button, but it took him about an hour to walk the length of himself. His speech was also affected, and he had a bit of a drawl. These were just physical impairments, however and, as I say, he was a really smart lad. He did well at school, and he actually came up with the basic idea for Sky Plus long before whoever Sky stole it from did. He didn't have the means to do anything with the concept, though. Sad.

Gooter wasn't worried about the boundaries that the rest of society placed upon him. He just got on with things. He was quite the ladies' man in his own way. In fact, that's how he got his nickname. 'Gooter' is a rather charming Irish slang term for vagina. 'My little Alfie just loves the minge,' his mum used to tell me proudly when I popped around to see Greg. And he did. He was a charming little bastard in his own right but, even so, all that my impetuous, adolescent eyes could see was a stuttering tortoise whose very existence was holding back this rapid young hare. Then something happened that completely obliterated my pathetic views.

We were all in the Tropical Sword one Friday night, as usual. The Bloody Marys were flowing and our young ears were being educated with the sheer musical innovation of 'Kung Fu Fighting' by Carl Douglas. We had our eyes on a group of young ladies on the other side of the bar, and everything was going swell. I had noticed, however, that a group of other lads in the club appeared to be sniggering in the direction of my posse. They were a rather rough, simple-looking bunch, and I imagined they had never seen a man of my size wearing a feather boa and a fedora before, so I ignored their laughable narrow-mindedness and carried on with my night. It soon became obvious, however, that they were laughing at Gooter. He teetered over to the cloakroom to hand in his jacket, and I watched as they nudged each other and guffawed. A young lad with a disability was trying to enjoy a night out, and these cretins were mocking him.

Part of me was furious, and I wanted to front up to the pricks and knock their bloomin' blocks off. 'Kung Fu Fighting' was still playing and I was pumped as fuck. Sadly, this protective side of me was overwhelmed by my immaturity. You see, I also became rather embarrassed. Embarrassed that someone that was in my company was there to be ridiculed like that. As I grew into the peacock I have become, I have learned to cherish and celebrate one's individuality, but back then I was just one of a million young men who didn't want to stick out.

I didn't do anything about the lads who made fun of Gooter. I didn't confront them or stick up for him in any way. I ignored it and joined the rest of my friends as they approached the young fillies at the other side of the nightclub. It was an act of cowardice that I've regretted ever since.

Gooter was blissfully unaware of the whole incident, and ended up fingering a girl in the disabled toilets later that night, so all's well that ends well, but the shame of my inaction has left a deep emotional scar that I have carried with me ever since.

These days, though, I am a different beast altogether. I embrace the differences in people, and I believe those who live with such difficulties should rise up against lazy preconceptions and naked insults, and integrate with the rest of society as easily and as freely as they possibly can. That's why, on the third Thursday of every month, I hit the town with Professor Stephen Hawking.

The professor and I became friends in 2002, when Bolton Wanderers sent me to a symposium on cosmology in Vienna. I've always suspected that the whole trip was a mistake on the part of the chairman's then new secretary, but the club insisted that I might learn a thing or two, so I decided to just go along with it. The conference was a bit of a disappointment – the views expressed on cosmology were rather redundant, I thought – but getting to know Hawking was an absolute delight. As we sat at the back of the conference hall, his robotic chants of 'BORRR-ING' aimed at each new speaker that got up on stage had me in stitches. We would stay up until the wee hours back at the hotel bar, righting the wrongs of the world and getting hammered on gin. There was a mix-up with my room, and I could only get one with a bunkbed, so the professor bunked in with me. It was like being a teenager again, having super fun sleepovers. He'd keep me up all night with filthy jokes and impressions of automotive navigation systems. Then, when he finally fell asleep, I'd gently wrap him up in a duvet, and toss him up to the top bunk like a bin bag.

Over the years, our friendship has grown. The professor has become an incredibly special friend, and someone whose opinion I truly cherish. He's also someone that I have a tremendous amount of respect for. Even as his condition continues to affect him and he increasingly resembles an oversized pretzel, he always stays positive, while his thirst for knowledge remains undiminished. He's also someone that refuses to let his disability define him.

A few years back, we began to meet up once a month. Nothing major, just a casual catch-up for a chat and a few laughs, seeing what was new with each other. We'd go for a cappuccino or catch a movie. I often suggested we head out for a nice meal, but he would always refuse.

'You. Don't. Want. To. Watch. Me. Eat. Big. Man,' he'd joke. 'I'm. Like. Fucking. Brundlefly.'

Eventually, though, we got a little bit more daring and started going for a pint or two. Ste was in his absolute element. He loved everything about being in a bar; the touch of the oak, the smell of the beer, the hum of laughter and chat. I got him one of those novelty beer hats off eBay. I'd place a couple of cans of ale into the holders, pop the straws into his mouth and away we'd go. Watching him get tipsy was a strange sort of joy. Just seeing this master of physics let his hair down, and become one of the rabble was both beautiful and humbling. I had to reprimand him once when he'd had a bit too much La Chouffe and chanted, 'Get. Your. Gums. Around. My. Plums' at what he thought was a woman, but turned out to be a man who was clearly still clinging to glam metal, but all in all, Hawking was good as gold.

The pub we went to most frequently had a belting jukebox and Ste was in love with it. 'Play. Some. Dire. Straits,' he'd roar, as I perused its offerings. We'd sit all night, downing neck oil and dancing like fuck in our seats. It was, in retrospect, a very obvious precursor to the next stage of our social evolution: hitting a nightclub.

The first time I took the professor to a nightclub was one of the most emotional moments of my life. My eyes stayed firmly on his face as he zoomed in and was exposed to the neon-lit brilliance of the place. I couldn't help but be transported back 45 years to the night I first walked into the Tropical Sword. Sure, the music was different, the fashion more daring and everyone was on cocaine, but the sheer thrill of such sensory overload remained the same. The professor's eyes widened. He was like that little stinker Charlie when he first entered Willy Wonka's chocolate factory. As I got us a couple of drinks, however, I noticed Ste's head was bowed and the smile had vanished from his face. Well, I think it had; it's hard to read his expressions, to be honest. It's why he's such a devastating poker player.

'What's up, prof?' I asked.

'This,' he said, coldly.

'What?'

'This.'

'Sorry, Ste, I don't know if you think you're motioning or pointing towards something, but you're not, pal.'

'This. Thiiiiiiis. This. Machine. That. Confines. Me.'

I looked at his wheelchair. This instrument of metal and wire that had caged him for decades.

'It's. Okay. In. A. Pub. But. How. Can. I. Enjoy. Myself. In. A. Place. Like. This?' he asked.

A smug grin spread across myself. I had anticipated this problem. I didn't want Ste to watch from the sidelines. I wanted him to have the ultimate nightclub experience, and the trip I made to Mothercare the previous day would ensure he had just that. I winked at the professor as I reached inside my back-pack and pulled out a gorgeous, three-position baby carrier. He looked back at me blankly.

'What. Is. That?' he asked. 'I. Thought. You. Brought. Red. Bull. In. That. Bag.'

'Always two steps ahead, Ste,' I said. 'Always two steps ahead.'

I threw my head back wildly and laughed the laugh of cunning invention. I then lifted him from his wheel-chair, popped him into the baby carrier and strapped him to my chest. I turned and faced the dancefloor. Motor neurone disease had robbed my friend of the chance to experience a million things that you or I take for granted. But not tonight. Tonight, he would experience what everybody who stepped into a nightclub came to experience. Tonight, he would dance.

Right at that moment, the familiar beat of the Linn LM-1 drum machine exploded out of the speakers, as 'Delirious' by the late, great Prince began to play. I looked at the professor and smiled. Oh, it was on.

I trotted towards the dancefloor with gay abandon, like a mighty silverback gorilla carrying his young. We hit the dancefloor just as that glorious keyboard hook kicked in. The revellers parted like the Red Sea, scores of punters staring at us in stunned silence. As the music took over my body, the professor and I became one. A bit like Krang from *Teenage Mutant Ninja Turtles* with his human-shaped exo-suit.

We danced for 90 minutes straight and lost ourselves completely to the vibe, as well as the ecstasy that we bought from a curvy young girl called Barbara. I got a little bit carried away when Timberlake's 'Sexy-Back' came on and pulled Ste out of the baby carrier before swinging him around my head like a kettlebell but, aside from that one misstep, it was one of the most intensely enjoyable evenings we've ever spent together. I even had a slow dance with Barbara right at the end of the night, just so the professor could nestle his sweaty little face right between her magnificent top bollocks.

As we headed for the exit door, the professor had a look of pure joy etched on his face. He had never looked happier. I was dying to hear his thoughts on the evening, but I needed to hook him back up to his computer before I could. Unfortunately, some cunt had nicked his wheelchair. Thankfully, I found an unattended girl's bike outside the club, so I popped him into the basket and began the long journey home.

The streets were filled with clubbers. As I cycled past one particular group, a drunken lout shouted 'ET phone home!' at us. I contemplated ignoring him, but the image of Gooter Daly came crashing back into my head. I couldn't let this happen again. I leapt off the bike and attacked the group with all the ferocity of a tiger. After dispensing with the rest, my eyes settled on the lad who had insulted my friend. He could barely look me in the eye, his body trembling with fear.

'Jesus, mate, I was only messing,' he slurred. 'You're riding a bike with a dog in the basket. It's like ET, for fuck's sake. I didn't mean no harm.'

'That is no dog, hombre,' I replied firmly. 'That is Professor Stephen Hawking. That is Gooter Daly. That is the girl that used to be in *Grange Hill*. That is every person with a disability that cunts like you have ever laughed it. And this? This is your reckoning.'

With that, I leapt at him, biting and scratching at him for a full four minutes. I honestly think I might have killed him, but one of his friends was able to pull him away just as I readied myself to clamp down on his jugular. As they ran into the night like cowards, I looked to the stars and sobbed. I might never rid myself of the shame I still feel for turning my back on Gooter, but right at that moment, I felt some sort of atonement. That deep, emotional scar was still there, but suddenly it didn't feel quite as raw.

Unfortunately, I was so enraged by the heckling that started that whole thing, that I jumped off the bike before it came to a full stop and so it crashed into a canal with the professor still in the basket. Thankfully, he got lodged inside an old tyre which prevented him from coming to a watery end. I managed to fish him out, but he didn't talk to me for months afterwards. He came round eventually, though. He always does.

And Gooter? I don't keep in touch with him anymore, but I hope he's doing well. I hope he's happy and successful but, above all, I hope he dances. I hope he dances long into the night and suckles at the very teat of human experience, for no matter who we are or what 'burdens' we may carry, it remains the finest milk any of us shall ever drink.

# What I Would do if I Had Five Minutes in a Room With Jimmy Savile

Back in 2000, I attended a fundraiser for the campaign to get Nestle to bring back the Secret Bar, in a glitzy hotel in London. The Secret was perhaps the most luxurious chocolate bar of the 1990s, featuring delicate strands of milk chocolate over a light, creamy mousse filling. It was the Rolls-Royce Phantom Coupé of confectionery, but just like the Coupé, it cost an absolute bomb to manufacture and it was eventually discontinued. Nothing gets British blood pumping quite like very trivial things, so I was very happy to help out with the campaign, even though I really didn't give a fuck.

Despite my apathy, the fundraiser was a roaring success, and the hotel was replete with genuine A-list celebrities. The Kemp brothers were there, along with Emma Forbes, Trevor Francis, Ian McShane and the Super Furry Animals. Despite my rather lacklustre expectations, the night also turned out to be a huge amount of fun. Forbesy was at her flirtatious best, while the Kemp brothers had everyone in stitches with their tales of 1980s' pop excess during their time in Spandau Ballet. Did you know that on one occasion, lead singer Tony Hadley wolfed down so much cocaine before a gig in Weston-super-Mare that he actually began to think he was Simon Le Bon, singing Duran Duran lyrics over each of the arrangements at the concert? Fucking mad.

All was going well until shortly after midnight. The event was starting to wind down and people were leaving. Those that remained relaxed at the bar, indulging in one last brandy before calling it a night. All was quiet when, seemingly out of nowhere, we began to hear a faint jangling noise from the hallway outside the bar. We didn't think much about it at first but, as it got louder and more ominous, we all started to get a little bit spooked. If we were in a horror movie, this would have been either the moment when the monster revealed itself for the first time, or it would be a tense, suspenseful build-up that eventually made way for sheer relief, as a friendly face popped his or her head around the corner. In reality, the scenario was somewhere in between. The jangling was coming from a chunky, nine-carat gold identity bracelet that was clanking against a similarly-gaudy, diamond-encrusted watch that draped off the wrist of one James Wilson Vincent Savile.

I'd grown up with Jimmy Savile on the television but, unlike millions of others across the United Kingdom, I was never a fan. I viewed him as a rather peculiar character. There was always something slightly unsettling about his mannerisms, tics, voice, clothes, trainers and hair. Despite my lukewarm feelings about him and the fact that his appalling tracksuits virtually screamed, 'I am a fucking threat to you,' I never really gave him any serious thought and certainly didn't consider him as someone with genuine malevolence. Don't get me wrong, I wouldn't have ever wanted to have a pint with him, and I wouldn't leave him alone in a room with a hollowed-out melon, never mind another man, woman or child, but I just assumed he was a slightly creepy old man, even when he was young, and nothing more. There were certainly always rumours surrounding him, but I really didn't imagine he could be the utter fiend we now know he was. My suspicions, however, were certainly aroused a little more when I met him that night.

Savile, we found out later, was staying at the hotel and – him being the king of charity and all that – he had dropped into the bar when the receptionist told him a fundraiser had taken place earlier in the night. The first thing you should understand about Savile was the downright squalor of his physical appearance. I'm not sure television every truly did it justice. He looked like the Crypt Keeper from *Tales from the Crypt*. Well, he would if that cackling little ghoul bought all his clothes from MandM Direct and washed his face with turpentine. Honestly, he looked like shit. Every last part of his body looked like it could fall off at any given time. It was hard not to hide your disgust when you were just a few metres away from the man.

He slithered up to us at the bar, his brown – yes, fucking brown – shell-suit making a hideous tinfoil-like swishing sound as he walked. 'Now, then,' he said, predictably. 'A little birdie tells me that you boys and girls are trying to raise money to bring back a delicious chocolate bar, is that right?' It was just me, Gary Kemp and BBC royal correspondent Nicholas Witchell at the bar by this stage, so I don't know why he said, 'Boys and girls'. 'I think that's a marvellous idea,' he continued, his shit jewellery jingling all over the place as he gesticulated wildly. 'I'm doing a charity walk to raise money for a local dog hospital tomorrow morning. Lovely, lovely dogs, with no legs. No legs at all. Just little doggie bodies and lovely little doggie heads. Need money to build them some legs. The hospital gets on the phone – the phone – to Jimmy. "Say no more," says I. "I'll get you that money. Don't you worry about that, sunshines."'

Just to reiterate, the man looked absolutely ghastly in the flesh, and the three of us were having difficulty doing anything other than staring at him intently. We were unable to even acknowledge what he had just said, never mind offer a retort. Eventually, I shook myself out of my repulsed reverie, and sprang into glib action. 'They've got Pringles behind the bar,' I said. 'Get four of them for each mutt. They'll do. They just have the small cans, mind, but beggars can't be choosers.'

Savile looked back at me, completely nonplussed. He smiled that horrible smile for pretty much every photograph he ever posed for, but he was never a man of humour. He took another suck on his horrid, wet little cigar. 'I'll get them the money,' he said eventually, ignoring my quip. 'Now then, here then, why then, there then, I'll get them the money for the little doggies. Jim'll fix it, boys and girls. He always does.'

At that point, his creepy little bumbag burst open, and dozens of Tamagotchis fell out. Dozens of them, all the colours of the rainbow. I looked at Kemp and Witchell. Three of our combined six eyebrows arched in unison. Savile bent down and casually lifted each Tamagotchi up and popped them back into his fanny pack. Carrying all these toys around on his person was a sizeable enough red flag as it was but, when he bent down, his tracksuit top pulled up, and I could see he was wearing Speedo swimming trunks under his bottoms with the 'S' in the logo scribbled out with a felt-tip pen. I mean, come on, FFS.

By now, I really just wanted to get away from him. Kemp made his excuses and left, while Witchell had already made clear earlier in the evening his determination to go to a titty bar. I was just about to tell Savile we had to leave when he saved me the hassle, saying he was tired and was retiring to his room. Before he left, he shook my hand – a two-handed handshake, of course, another fucking red flag – and told me to 'be a good boy, or else the bogeyman will get you'. He then slithered back out of the bar and towards the elevator. As he did so, I noticed his footwear for the first time. LA Lights. Red flags all over the fucking shop.

That was the first and only time I was ever in the company of Jimmy Savile and, frankly, that one occasion was more than enough. A few months later, Louis Theroux's documentary on him was aired, and everyone began to see the man in a much more sinister light. Fast-forward 17 years, and the full, horrifying details of what kind of predator he was are well-known to everyone. He was a fucking rotter. There's little point going over his litany of vile crimes. We're all aware of what he did, and we all feel utterly nauseated that he got away with; even those that were aware of what he was doing at the time. One thing has always persisted at the back of my mind, though. What if I knew what Jimmy Savile was guilty of when I met him back in 2000 at that London hotel? What if I knew what he was up to, and I could have had five minutes alone in a room with him to administer the punishment he so richly deserved? The punishment that he evaded through his life? I've ran this through my mind a million times in the years that have passed, and I think it would probably go a little something like this...

I watch as Savile enters the elevator. 'Look at the state of his LA-fucking-Lights,' I say to Witchell. 'What a fucking creep.' Witchell is drunk by now. Real drunk. All he wants is tits in his face. I tell him he'll have to hit the strip clubs on his own. I have a nonce to destroy.

I go to reception and ask them what room Savile is in. Predictably, they tell me they can't give me that kind of information. 'Really?' I say with a smirk then, all of a sudden, I'm wearing tight denim shorts and my ass looks like a million-fucking-dollars in them. I turn around and show her the goods.

'He's in room 165, sweet cheeks,' says the receptionist breathlessly. I give her a wink, then head for the stairs. 'The elevator is right there, sir,' says the receptionist.

'How do you think I keep my ass in such good shape?' I reply, and throw in another wink for good measure.

She throws her head back and laughs manically. I'll remember this girl for later. She has moxie.

I walk up to the first floor and find room 165 with ease. I take a deep breath then knock on the door, slowly and deliberately. Savile opens the door. He's wearing a dressing robe and a pair of jelly sandals. Yellow jelly sandals. My urge to murder him immediately is off the fucking scale.

'Now, then, now, then,' he says. Again. Change the record, you fucking pervert. 'What have we here?'

'JUSTICE!' I scream, before I kick him in the stomach and send him sprawling to the other side of the room. As he recoils in horror, I walk in calmly, and shut the door behind me. Savile squirms on the ground. Like a worm. 'You fucking worm,' I spit at him perceptively.

'What's ... what's this ... all about, boys and girls?' he pleads.

I pull him up by the hair and pin him to the wall. I punch him 47 times in the face with my fist, which has become steel, like Fisto's from *He-Man and the Masters of the Universe*. Unsurprisingly, Savile's face is now a mangled mess. It's like a big, pink blancmange with a shit wig plopped atop it. I pull him towards me by the lapels, bringing his wretched face close to the chiselled magnificence of my own. 'What do you have to say for yourself, shit-bird?' I bark.

'I like your denim shorts,' he replies, blood dripping from his vile, crooked mouth.

I slap him about the neck and face 64 more times, this time with my other hand which has become a frying pan. It's like a terrifying edition of *Shooting Stars*. When I'm done, I throw him into the ceiling fan. He whirls around for ages, screaming like a fucking bell-end. Both of his arms come off.

Try groping young 'uns now, dirtbag, I think to myself. I don't say it out loud, though. It's not a time for my patented quippery.

Eventually, he drops to the ground. His whimpers grow louder and louder. I pick him up by the balls. 'This is your last chance to repent,' I say. 'Don't you have anything to say about your crimes?'

He looks at me blankly, and takes a draw from his cigar. I really don't know how he managed to take a puff, in all honesty, as he has no fucking arms, but I ignore it and stare back. He leans in to my ear. He's so busted up he can barely breathe, never mind talk, but he clearly wants to say something. I listen carefully as he struggles to speak. These may be his final words. Will he make them count?

'Jim'll fix it for you and you and ... bah-bah-bah,' he sings, before laughing his head off.

I scream in anger and throw him back up into the ceiling fan. His legs come off this time. Fucking brilliant. I reach up and grab him. I've got Inspector Gadget-like arms now, so I can easily reach. I pull him down and hang him on a hook on the wall. A hook that's reserved for beautiful art, not disgusting sexual predators. I look at what's left of him. A bloodied torso and a battered face. I pull my trusty sword, Trudy, from her sheath on my back. I examine the steel of the blade. Cool, clean, sharp. I kiss Trudy and hold her aloft, high above my head.

'BY THE POWER INVESTED IN ME BY THE PEOPLE OF BRITAIN,' I roar, 'I HEREBY SENTENCE YOU TO THE DEATH YOU SO RICHLY DESERVE!'

I chop off his grim little penis and glue it to his forehead.

'You fucking dickhead!' I scream, looking at his face one last time. There's not one ounce of remorse in those abject, lifeless eyes. I bow my head and summon the power of a thousand unheard voices. It is all the power I need for my final strike.

'Shoryuken!' I roar, before executing a perfect Rising Dragon Fist (Ken's, not Ryu's) on him. The majesty of my strike has taken his head clean off his fucking shoulders. Savile is dead. I kick his already rotting skull out the window and watch it splash into the River Thames. I watch as it floats off into the night. Into the darkness.

Jimmy Savile has been completely and utterly demolished by my own hands. No. By the hands of the people he wronged. The hands of the people of this great nation, who took him into their hearts and considered him to be some sort of kindly, television uncle. He hoodwinked and betrayed those people and thought he would get away with it. Not on my watch, though. On my watch, he doesn't get a park bench dedicated to his memory. He doesn't get a plaque. He doesn't get an inclined coffin in the cemetery so his shrivelled corpse can look out to the sea. In my world, he gets torn apart like rancid fudge, his head bobbling lifelessly down the Thames with his own shit cock glued to his forehead. How very fucking fitting.

I put Trudy back into her sheath and leave the room. I head back down to the hotel lobby to strike up a conversation with that cute receptionist. I have lots of ice-breakers; I've just killed Britain's most notorious sex offender and one of my hands is a frying pan. Perhaps I'll take her to a strip club where we can laugh at Nicholas Witchell and his pathetic attempts to charm a stripper. Or perhaps I'll take her home and make sweet, fully consensual love to her. Because that's what I am. A gentleman. A gentleman who knows right from wrong.

Of course, none of this happened. I never got a chance to wreak vengeance on Jimmy Savile. None of us did. But how many times have you said you'd give anything to have five minutes alone with someone you revile? I know I've said it a million times about some of history's greatest villains. Jimmy Savile, Hitler, Charles Manson, Normski. I've fantasised about eviscerating all of them. Would I really do it if I had the chance, though? Would any of us? Even if we did, would it actually make us feel better? Would it do any good? Would this kind of brutal, vigilante justice help heal the Britain that has been broken by monsters like Jimmy Savile?

I really don't know the answers to any of these questions. All I know is that I enjoyed killing Jimmy Savile in my fantasy, but I'm not sure that society would be ready to thank me for it. Yet again, Big Sam is the hero this country deserves, but probably not the one it needs right now.

The Secret bar still hasn't returned, by the way. It really is like pissing into the fucking wind at times.

# How
# to Deal
# With an
# Online Troll

The internet is a truly remarkable place. From the moment you connect, you are merely taps on a keyboard away from the largest treasure trove of information and stimulation that has ever been amassed. From biographies of famous Russian novelists to videos of strangers having sex without condoms, it's all there – if you know where to look.

Getting online can also offer you endless forms of entertainment, the ability to connect with people from every corner of the globe and a platform to shop for any product you can dream of without needing to leave your home. It doesn't matter if you get on using an AOL CD or visit a dingy internet cafe alongside a bunch of smiling Africans; if you're able to get online, you are part of a seamlessly connected world of limitless possibilities.

The internet, however, is not without its pitfalls. Phishing attacks, chatroom perverts and your racist uncle joining Facebook are just a few of the very real dangers out there in cyberspace, and every single one of them will target you if you fail to protect yourself adequately. There is one online menace, however, that seems able to roam the information superhighway, inflicting pain and anguish on innocent bystanders, without any sort of consistent retribution. This threat can strike in any corner of the internet. It doesn't want your money, your personal details or pictures of your balls or fanny. It only wants to harass. Waging a sustained war on faceless strangers for its own amusement is the only plunder interesting this recreant. This is the internet troll – and the hateful little spunk-bags are everywhere.

We all know the singular aim of the internet troll; to derail conversation by posting inflammatory, sarcastic or insulting remarks, purely to intimidate or upset other internet users. They can pop up anywhere; under a YouTube video, in the bowels of a dank online forum or under the byline of any story that appears in the *Daily Mail*. Their natural habitat, however, is increasingly becoming the vast, rocky landscape of social media.

Facebook, Bebo and MySpace are all replete with bell-ends, but if you really want to find a true internet troll in his purest form, the Twitter is the place to go. I got myself a Twitter account a few years ago, after being turned on to it by big Christopher Samba while I was at Blackburn Rovers. Chrissy predicted the platform would soon be the primary source for news and opinion on the internet and I should jump aboard. He also claimed the place was absolutely teeming with naked women desperate to share erotic images of themselves.

'I use Twitter for wanks,' he said brusquely, as we sat down for breakfast at the Rovers' training ground one morning. He then lifted his sleeve and showed me a freshly, bleeding tattoo that read 'Twitter 4 Wanx'. I'd heard enough. Twitter was clearly the place to be, and I wanted in on it.

Instead of using Twitter to consume information, however, I've actually been much more interested in the opposite; I wanted to use it as a platform to spread the wisdom and insight that I have spent decades accumulating. I wanted to bridge the gap to my legions of fans, and speak to them directly, from the heart. I don't use the Twitter much these days but it's always there, waiting for me to pounce if I want to communicate something to a wider audience. At the time, I took to the Twitter with aplomb and quickly established myself as one of the leading thinkers on the platform.

One night back in 2015, however, opened my eyes to another side of the Twitter. A darker, uglier side. I had just left my job at West Ham and I was in another period of professional limbo. Being able to speak to my fans online was a tremendous boon in a terribly difficult period. Unemployment is lonely and being able to connect was a vital part in my attempts to keep my mind sharp and my spirits high.

It was around 10.30 pm and I was sat on my sofa, watching *No Retreat, No Surrender* with a cool can of Dale's Pale Ale. I casually flicked on my WAP-enabled telephone and checked my Twitter page. I didn't notice anything unusual at first; just a few comments from well-wishers, hoping to see me back in the Premier League soon. I was about to put my phone down and carry on with the movie when something caught my eye. It was a comment from someone calling himself @FartMan69, and it stabbed into me like a hot knife through emotional butter: 'Your know good at football manager and i wish ur ma did abortion on her muff when you in it'.

I sat in silence and stared at the vile words for a good minute or so, as a tear trickled down my face. It was like that bit in *The Elephant Man* when Dr Treves is exposed to Merrick for the first time and sees what a truly fucking dreadful state he's in. It's the moment when he finally realises just how appalling human nature can be.

I was as confused by @FartMan69's words as I was hurt. Why would anyone indulge in such a heinous, unprovoked attack on a public forum? I'm not ashamed to admit I was a little bit shaken. I'm usually fairly robust, and very capable of taking on the challenge of a verbal assailant, but the sheer spite on show unsettled me and so I decided to simply ignore it. That's the consensus when dealing with trolls, isn't it? Ignore them. Starve them of the attention they are clearly after. I put down my phone and carried on with my evening.

Fast-forward to around 3 am, and I'm halfway through *No Retreat, No Surrender 3: Blood Brothers*. The action was coming thick and fast, so I decide to take a break and get some refreshments. I was all out of Dale's Pale Ale, so I made myself a White Russian and grabbed some Oreos for good measure. I checked my phone again. The wife had popped around to her accountant's for some money advice at around 9 pm, but there were no texts from her. She must have decided to sleep over again. I decided to check my Twitter page one more time before getting back to the movie. I logged in and noticed I had one new reply. Who could it be from?

It was @FartMan69 again, of course, and this time he was telling me that I look like the 'spasmo brother in *There's Something About Mary*' and that I should 'give up football and become a full-time queer because you are a queer'.

I threw the White Russian against the wall and crushed the Oreos into my own face. I attempted an angry retort but I was literally shaking with rage so my comment was riddled with grammatical errors and barely made any sense. @FartMan69 replied almost instantaneously. 'LOL @ u. u cant hardly write but its hard to write when u got u hands on ur boyfriends big fat dick. Delete ur account.'

I fell to my knees, devastated. 'I don't have a boy-friend!' I squealed in anguish. At this point, Iain Dowie interjected. I probably should have mentioned that Iain Dowie had been sat beside me in the room the whole time. We love to watch movies together. He's really into his martial arts flicks, and had been banging on about the *No Retreat, No Surrender* trilogy for months.

'What's wrong, champ?' he asked. I showed him the messages. 'Good grief,' he said, as he pored over @Fart Man69's filth. 'He doesn't even have a profile picture. Just one of those eggs. A sure sign of a troubled mind.'

I explained how I'd tried to ignore him without success and that my attempts to engage with the troll just seemed to push him into even nastier terrain. 'What should I do, Dowsie?' I asked, pleadingly.

Iain stood up and thrust his finger into the air dramatically. 'To the laboratory!' he shouted.

I looked back at him blankly. I didn't have a labora-tory. I'm a football manager, not a scientist.

'Your computer room, champ,' he clarified. 'Let's pop up to your computer room.'

At this point, I should point out that Dowsie is a genius. A bona fide fucking genius. He might look a bit like Earthworm Jim, but inside that big melon head resides a quite brilliant brain. He's got a degree in engineering and once received a personal tour of the Teletext offices, after getting a perfect score on *Bamboozle!* 19 days in a row. I stood behind him as he sat down at the computer and sprang into action. His fingers seemed to tap at the keys with the speed of lightning. It was like something from *A Beautiful Mind*. I imagined invisible fractions and formulas floating around Iain's head as he continued to work. He was drooling a little bit as he often does when he's not talking but, by Christ, he looked impressive.

As he finished whatever it was he was doing, he tapped the enter key with a dramatic flourish, and leaned back in his chair. A ream of text appeared on the screen.

'There you go,' he said, with a smirk. 'He's all yours.'

I took a closer look. 'What is it?' I asked.

'It's @FartMan69. His name, address, date of birth – heck, I've even got his passport number.'

My mouth dropped to the floor. I knew Iain was smart, but I didn't know he could do this sort of thing. It was all so ... dangerous. 'Are you a hacker?' I asked.

Iain shrugged his shoulders, his smirk widening.

'Jesus, this is just like *The Matrix* or something,' I said, giddily.

'The what?' asked Iain.

'*The Matrix.*'

'Is that a wrestler?'

'No, Iain. The film, *The Matrix.* You must have heard of *The Matrix?*'

'Well, I'm telling you I haven't. It sounds shite.'

'For fuck's sake, Iain, why are you only interested in martial arts films? There's loads of other genres.'

'Oh, really? And how is this *Matrix* shite going to help me if I'm being pursued by rapists?'

'Christ, Iain, why are you always going on about having to repel rapists? Have you been raped?'

'Yes.'

'Wait, what?'

'Well, no, but someone could try. And if they do … '

Dowsie then stood up and began to do a few karate moves while emitting some, frankly rather racist, Asian-sounding grunts. I told him to forget about martial arts movies and being raped, and explain how he got @FartMan69's details. I didn't really follow it fully, but it seems he broke into the mainframe and obtained the user's IP address. This, in turn, allowed him to ascertain the address from which the messages were sent. He then used the address on one of the internet explorers and was able to discover @FartMan69's real name and date of birth. He was 36-year-old Chris Peacock, from Croydon, south London.

'This is incredible,' I said. 'What do we do now?'

'Whatever you want, chief,' said Iain. 'I'm jumping into the dark web here to buy more dick tablets from Hong Kong. You go downstairs and have a think about what you want to do.'

I sat in the living room for 20 minutes pondering just that. Should I report Peacock to the police? Or expose him on the Twitter and let my legion of fans defend my honour by harassing him? Should I go even further and pay him a visit? I wanted revenge, I knew that, but I really didn't know how far I was prepared to go.

Eventually, Iain came back downstairs. 'Made your decision?' he asked.

I looked at him coldly, trying to generate a moral judgement in my mind. I opened my mouth, not even knowing what I was about to say. Whatever came out, I would abide by. 'I want retribution, Iain Dowie, and I want it now.'

'Excellent,' he replied archly, 'to the laboratory!'

I looked at him blankly again.

'My car,' he explained. 'Let's get into my car and go visit the little cunt.'

'Why do you call everything "the laboratory"?'

'Dunno. It's funny. Saw it in a film once.'

'Oh, and what martial arts film was that? Did Chuck Norris make one in the 1980s called *To The Laboratory*?'

'I've seen other types of films, all right? I just happen to prefer … '

'Oh, fuck this, Iain, let's just go … '

And with that, we were off. It was around 3.30 am, and the streets of London Town were empty. I gazed out of the window as Iain cruised towards our destination. At several points in the journey I wanted to tell him to just turn around, but the words wouldn't come out. Perhaps it was destiny. Perhaps I needed to deal with this troll. Not just for his abuse of me – I'd heard worse from the stands every week – but in response to the abuse of every person without a voice, those who had gone online to talk to friends or discuss politics and been on the receiving end of mindless vitriol.

We got to the address and parked outside. It was a grubby little house in a grubby little street. I took a deep breath and got out of the car.

'Want me to come with you, champ?' asked Iain.

'No, pal,' I replied. 'You hang back. This is on me.'

I walked towards the door, my entire body tingling. I had goosebumps over every inch of my skin and, for some reason, an absolutely honking erection. I still didn't know what I'd do if he answered the door, but I was excited. Being out of work does a lot of things to a man, and robbing him of the thrill that life can give you in these small moments is one of them. You feel too useless to get them.

I got to the door and knocked on it. It was after 4 am and I really didn't think anyone would answer. I was about to turn and walk back to the car when the door opened slowly. A small, chunky man in a *Star Wars* T-shirt and dressing gown stood peering out at me.

'Yeah? he said slowly. He had a thick beard and stank of cigarette smoke. He also had big man-tits and was probably a virgin.

'Chris Peacock?' I asked.

'Who wants to know?' he drawled.

'Does this ring any bells?'

I thrust my phone towards him, pushing his own vile words into his face.

'A dog in a cape?' he replied.

I turned the phone around and looked at it. I'd opened up Instagram instead by mistake. A really adorable dog account I follow. Some of the pics are absolutely hilarious. I quickly navigated back to the Twitter and showed him his messages.

'What … are you … how did you find me?' he spluttered.

'I have my ways.'

'You also seem to have a boner.'

It was still there, for fuck's sake. I tried to tuck it between my legs, but to no avail. 'Don't you worry about that, fat chops. Just worry about me. Why did you send me those messages? Why hate on a brother like that?'

He looked utterly ashamed. His gaze dropped to the floor. He began to spin some sorry excuse about wanting to lash out at a world that had turned its back on him. I almost began to pity him. Maybe it was just a cry for attention. Maybe he was just as much of a victim in all of this as I was. Then I remembered he said I looked like the retarded brother in *There's Something About Mary* and rage flowed through my body like lava. I lifted him up and suplexed him to the pavement.

He squealed in agony. 'I'll report you to the League Manager's Association!' he shouted as I rained blows down upon him.

'Good luck, they don't even have a fucking email address!' I cackled, before picking him up and smashing his face against a parked Citroën Saxo. I finished destroying him then tossed him back into his grotty little house. At that moment, Iain came running over and began to lay down some karate moves again. They looked pretty good, to be fair.

'Need any help, boss?' he asked.

'All done, son,' I replied. 'All done.' I checked the troll wasn't dead before closing the front door and heading back to the car. We didn't speak a word for the entire journey back to my house.

Was I wrong to do what I did? I don't know. Did it feel good? A little. Do I look like that simple lad with the ear-muffs in *There's Something About Mary?* I hope not.

The journey back seemed to take forever, but we got home eventually. Iain looked at me. The only thing in the world I wanted from him right at that moment was to *not* talk about what I'd just done. 'So,' he said, a solemn look etched on his face. 'I have *Big Trouble in Little China* in the glove compartment if you fancy it.' His face broke into a grin. I'd love to say it was a beautiful grin but, come on – we all know what he looks like. Still, at that moment, in the early morning as we sat outside my gaff in Iain Dowie's car, I could have kissed him.

'Definitely!' I said, before thrusting my finger into the air. 'To the laboratory!' We burst into laughter, before going back inside and watching the movie.

Because that's what it's all about, folks. Spending quality time with the people you love, making memories and having fun. Internet trolls really aren't worth the energy. Think of them as pesky little flies, desperately jockeying for your attention as you enjoy a delicious picnic with friends on a hot summer's day. Why would you ignore the food on offer, the company and the beautiful weather to focus on an insignificant little bug that can be easily swatted away? Life is too short, my friends. Life is too short.

Chris Peacock, 36, died of unrelated injuries a year after this incident. May he rest in peace.

# Is Dreaming of Making Love to an Animal Wrong?

*'...I have a dream that one day every valley shall be exalted, every hill and mountain shall be made low. The rough places will be made plain and the crooked places will be made straight. And the glory of the Lord shall be revealed, and all flesh shall see it together.'*

Martin Luther King Jr. uttered these beautiful words on the steps of the Lincoln Memorial in Washington DC on 28 August 1963. The great man had a dream that one day his homeland would be free from racial intolerance, and the freedom of every man, woman and child would be cherished and upheld, regardless of the colour of their skin.

Far be it from me to compare myself to Dr King – although I find it hard to believe he wouldn't have been in awe of the job I did with Bolton, not to mention being pretty damn impressed with just how effortlessly I got on with Jay-Jay Okocha – but I too have a dream. It may not be as lofty as King's, but it is one that I truly believe is just as thought-provoking. For a while now I've been having a very lucid, recurring dream in which I am having full penetrative sex with my childhood dog, Conker.

Before I go any further, let's just take a minute to exorcise the squalid pondering that, I have no doubt, is floating around your head right now. No, I did not have actual, real-life intercourse with Conker when he was alive. For fuck's sake. Conker was a companion and, yes, I did love him, but bestiality ain't my bag, man, and if it's your bag, then you need to get yourself a new bag, man, 'cos that bag ain't right. Now, back to the story …

On a cool spring day in 1964, Mother came home from her post-work pint holding a bag. There was nothing unusual in that, in all honesty, as she often came back from the pub with trinkets and treasures of differing shapes and sizes. One time, when I was very young, I remember her arriving home with a pristine prosthetic leg tucked under her arm.

'What's that, mama? Is that a leggy? Where'd you get that leggy from, mama?' I asked adorably as I tucked into my Fry's Chocolate Cream.

'I took it from a lady with diabetes because I *could*,' she replied defiantly, 'and if you keep eating chocolate the way you are, fat lad, I'll be fitting it onto your cellulite-ridden little stump in no time.'

As she entered the house on that day in 1964, however, something was a little amiss. I was in the living room, playing with my Slinky (there were no stairs in the living room, of course. In fact, there were no stairs anywhere in our house: we lived in a bungalow at that time. Mother had laughed hoarsely when I excitedly unwrapped the birthday paper to reveal a shiny new Slinky with wide-eyed excitement. 'Enjoy!' she roared, droplets of gin shooting out of her mouth).

As the room filled with the unmistakable stench of cigarillos and porter, I turned to say, 'Hello,' and noticed the bag. Probably just a big kettle, or some copper piping or something. No big deal. As I began to return to my Slinky, however, I noticed something from the corner of my eye. The bag had moved.

'That bag. It … it moved, Mama,' I said keenly.

'I know. There's a dog in it,' she replied. She wasn't really one for coating surprises with unnecessary drama.

'A doggie! For me?'

'Suppose so,' she said with a sigh. 'I was going to boil the little prick and chop him into a stew, but I can't be arsed now. This is your Christmas present, though. And you have to look after him. If I find lumps of his steamy shit anywhere in the house, I'll make you eat it, capiche?'

She then threw the bag on the sofa and sloped off to the kitchen to make herself a post-pub Boilermaker. The bag moved a little. Then a little more. I stood staring at it, joy and trepidation fighting for control in my little mind. I took another step forward. The bag barked! It was a deeper bark than I was expecting, but I ignored it and continued moving forward. After what felt like an age, I got to the sofa and peered into the bag. All I could see was darkness and then, out of nowhere, he appeared, jumping towards me like that cunt Gmork leaping at the boy-warrior Atreyu in the Swamps of Sadness near the end of Wolfgang Peterson's 1984 masterpiece, *The NeverEnding Story*. While Gmork's motives were murderous, as he strove to serve The Nothing in its evil attempts to engulf the magical world of Fantasia in sadness, the dog that jumped out at me had no such villainy in mind. Instead, he proceeded to paw me playfully, licking my face and wagging his tail. He then took an immediate shit on the floor. After lifting the offering up and throwing it out the window, I was able to get a proper look at my new pet for the first time. He was a beautiful brown labrador, with a mischievous grin and a grey beard. A very grey beard, in fact.

I walked into the kitchen, leaving my new pal to have a sniff of his new surroundings. Mother was sat at the table, getting stuck in to her second Boilermaker of the evening.

'Is he a puppy?' I asked.

'Who?

'My new doggie. He looks like a big puppy.'

'He looks about 15, you daft prick.'

'Where did you get him?'

'Saw him in a garden.'

'What's his name?'

'Fuck knows.'

'Can I call him Conker? He's the same colour as my conkers.'

Mother didn't answer. Instead, she slowly made a fist and started to form a thumbs-up. Then, at the last minute, she gave me the finger. I didn't mind, though. I had a new best friend, and I couldn't have been happier.

Conker only lived for another 18 months, but in that time we had more adventures than any pair of rascals could ever dream of. We ran carefree through summer meadows, splashed merrily down by the river and chased fireflies under the stars down by old man Huckleberry's farm. I even watched Conker eat an entire rat without chewing, out by the bins at the back of the local glue factory. Halcyon days. I've never had another friend quite like Conker, and I miss him to this day.

Fast-forward 40-odd years and Conker made an unexpected and somewhat curious return to my life. Soon after I was forced out of the England job, I began to suffer from stress, which in turn affected my sleep. I began lying awake all night, my brain going into overdrive, thinking about who had wronged me the most during the whole sorry episode, and unable to drift off.

The lack of sleep just added to my stress and the whole thing became a vicious circle.

I called my old, well-brewed-cup-of-tea-coloured pal David Dickinson for his advice. As one of Britain's most recognisable antique dealers, Dave is no stranger to stress. He once told some old woman that a little, crystal, owl-shaped brooch she had found in her attic might look like a real bobby-dazzler, but it was worth 'nowt but tuppence and a smile'. The old woman ended up giving it to her next door neighbour's granddaughter, who sold it for £1.2 million at auction. The granddaughter was a young Conservative as well, so you can imagine just how fucking sick the old woman felt. She ended up freezing to death the following winter. Dickinson felt rotten.

'Guilt consumed me like an illness, big man, and that guilt soon turned into stress,' he told me. 'I couldn't sleep for love nor money. The only thing that got me off was a bottle of Thunderbird and a handful of benzos. Cheap as chips at half the price.'

I took Dickinson's advice and finished each day with a safe, but potent, cocktail of cheap wine and sleeping pills to aid my interminable struggle with insomnia. This tactic seemed to do the trick, but there was a rather troublesome side effect; my dreams went fucking mental. I mean, proper David Lynch shit. Murder, violence, domination, dwarves. A succession of vivid, and sometimes disturbing, visions seeped into my unconscious mind each and every night. The only consistent aspect to each dream was the fact there *wasn't* any consistency.

Each nightfall seemed to bring with it a different nightmarish dreamscape to trap me as I slept. I decided that I needed to do something, so I upped the benzos. This seemed to do the trick in terms of stabilising the nature of my dreams. They became a little more sedate, and the themes stopped fluctuating so wildly. In fact, an air of regularity soon took hold. I began to dream about comparatively regular things. Sure, there was always the odd moment of surrealism thrown in but gone were the hideous dystopian visions that had been haunting me. Then, one night, after downing three bottles of Thunderbird and eating 37 Babybels, I laid my magnificent head down upon my John Lewis Canadian goose down pillow and began to dream about Conker.

The plot of the dream that evening was the same one that now unfolds every night. To the minutest detail. I'm at a hotel bar, a White Russian in one hand and a Fuente Fuente Opus X cigar in the other. The barman looks past me and motions. 'He's here, Mr President.'

I look behind me. Conker is there. 'He'll have a Rémy Martin,' I tell the barman.

Conker takes a seat beside me and begins slurping at the cognac when it comes.

'We have to stop meeting like this,' I say with a smirk. Conker doesn't respond. He's a dog, he can't. 'Did you bring what I asked?'

Bark!

'Come, come, Conker, you know why I asked you here.'

Bark! Bark!

'The microfilm, Conker. I want that microfilm.'

Conker looks away and begins lapping at the cognac again.

'Well, I see you're still quite the negotiator, even after all these years. How about we go up to my room and see if we can come to some sort of ... arrangement?'

At this stage Conker does a big shit on the ground. I lift it up and throw it out the window. We take the lift up to my room. It's on the 67th floor. Sixty-seven. My England reign lasted 67 days. Eventually, we get to my room.

'I'm going to have a quick shower, old friend. Why don't you ... make yourself more comfortable.'

Conker proceeds to do another shit on the floor.

'For fuck's sake, Conker!' I yell, my legendary cool leaving me for a moment. 'Stop shitting everywhere.'

I take a quick shower and towel myself off. I come back into the room. Conker is already in bed. He's eating one of my Fuente cigars. 'I see you've found my stash. I really should give up, shouldn't I? It's bad for my health. As are you.' With that, I drop my towel, exposing my taut, naked body. 'Perhaps this will help you remember where you put the microfilm.'

Bark!

'You like what you see, don't you? Let's give you a closer look.'

I move towards the bed then, for some reason, I suddenly lift my penis up with one hand, holding it like the neck of a guitar while strumming my scrotum with the other hand. I proceed to play a really elegant version of Fleetwood Mac's 'Never Going Back Again' as Conker continues to eat my expensive cigars like some sort of fucking savage.

'Did you enjoy that?' I say as I finish. 'That's "Never Going Back Again" played on my boner and balls. Just for you, Conker. Do you like how I play?'

Conker takes another shit. It's his third of the evening and, Jesus Christ, we only met about 15 minutes ago. I ignore it and slip into the bed. 'Let's not beat around the bush,' I say seductively.

Conker begins to pant.

'You're getting impatient. I like that. Tell me what you want, Conker.'

Conker howls like a feral wolf. I cock my head back and laugh like a fucking mentalist. I pull him towards me and gaze into his eyes. I hold the moment for a few seconds, eking out every last drop of drama. Then we kiss. Then we slowly, but very, *very* surely, make love. And not in a crude, doggie-style fashion; we do it in the traditional, missionary fashion, with Conker's paws draped around my neck. Yes, it is bestiality at the end of the day – you've got me bang to rights there – but it's also very tender. Then, right at the moment of climax, I wake up, screaming. And that's what I've been dreaming of, almost every single night, for the past six months.

I've spoken about this dream with some of my most astute and perceptive friends, including Steve Bruce, Barry Fry and Jim Davidson, but nobody can decipher its hidden meaning. Sigmund Freud – or Sigmund *Fraud*, as I call him – reckoned dreams could offer an insight into one's hidden desires and emotions. We can dismiss that claptrap immediately; I have no desire to bone a pooch, thank you very much. Freud did, however, also posit that dreams are manifestations of our deepest anxieties, and that they can be traced back to repressed childhood memories or obsessions.

I'm a popular guy but, as I said earlier, I've never really had a friend like Conker in the years since he passed. Perhaps these saucy dreams are merely my subconscious mind pining for that level of compan-ionship? Perhaps my grief for him runs deeper than I imagined, and I'm simply placing the two of us in the most intimate scenario two people can be a part of: the act of sexual congress. Or maybe I'm just angry at Mother for not stealing me a puppy and instead coming home with a fucking 15-year-old labrador that only lived for another year and a half.

The greatest minds on the planet still don't really know what dreams mean or where they come from, so who am I to quibble about my own nocturnal visions? Let's hope some other childhood trauma wriggles out of the woodwork at some time in the near future and that whatever new hell it is manifests itself in my dreams instead. To paraphrase the great Dr King once more, if and when that happens I will be free at last, free at last, thank God almighty, I'll be free at last.

# What Happens When You Fall in Love With Another Man?

It's 23 May 2004 and I'm chilling in my den at my home in Bolton, listening to The Streets' *A Grand Don't Come for Free* and blazing a blunt.

Back then, my man cave was the envy of the Premier League. It was a converted loft, split into zones and kitted out with every conceivable item the male heart could desire.

In the Sports Zone, I had a dartboard, a 4-foot snooker/pool table and a blow-football kit, while the Chillax Zone was replete with an imitation La-Z-Boy recliner, a beanbag and a lava lamp. The CZ – that's short for Chillax Zone – also doubled as the Snuggle Zone on the rare occasions when the wife was allowed into the den, and I fancied a bit of pork swordery of an evening.

The Refreshment Zone, meanwhile, had a mini-fridge full of fine craft ales and a black bin bag filled with beef Hula Hoops that I would replenish periodically. The Reading Zone had a book in it.

The most popular zone with guests, though, was without question the Entertainment Zone. The Entertainment Zone had it all: a Sharp LC-20AV6U 20-inch LCD TV – with infrared remote control and S-video input – a Sanyo MCD-XJ780 portable boombox with CD player and tape deck, a Toshiba DVD/VHS combo *and* a Nintendo GameCube with one controller. Phew!

'PC World for tramps,' Stuart Pearce called it. Classic fucking Stu, that. Always with the jokes.

I would spend countless hours in my den, either on my own or with friends, playing *Mario Kart*, blazing blunts and generally getting my chill on. It offered respite from the pressures of managing in the Premier League and from modern life in general. No matter what was happening at Bolton Wanderers, how angry the psoriasis around my inner thighs was getting or how threatening the letters I received from the Britannia Music Club were, I could always rely on the sanctuary of my man cave to block out the darkness and to keep me feeling safe and warm.

On that particular Sunday evening back in 2004, however, I wasn't feeling all that splendid. A few months earlier, I had taken my Bolton team to Wembley to compete in the League Cup final, against Steve McClaren's Middlesbrough. The game had extra importance, as it marked my first appearance at a domestic cup final as a player or manager. It was a chance for me to take my rightful place at the very top of modern football and cement my reputation as one of the game's true innovators.

Before the game, I told my players that I alone would be lifting the trophy. They understood. It was, after all, what the world had been waiting for. Big Sam, after a lifetime of being the prettiest bridesmaid at the wedding, finally getting his hands on some silverware. They weren't quite as understanding when I told them that I would also be taking each one of their winners' medals so I could melt them down and forge myself a giant collar with regal livery, but they could go fuck themselves, quite frankly.

In the end, none of it mattered anyway. We lost the game 2–1, with the decisive goal coming as a result of a disgraceful penalty decision. To rub salt into my gaping wounds, referee Mike Riley also failed to give my side a penalty late in the game, despite a clear handball by a Boro defender in the penalty area. The big fucking pervert.

As I sat solemnly in the dressing room afterwards, listening to the Middlesbrough fans celebrating wildly in the stadium, I felt as sad as I've ever been. I was as blue as a poofter at a rodeo. My big Brazilian defender Emerson Thome sidled up to me and put his arm around my shoulder.

'Hey, boss,' he garbled, his thick, South American accent both charming and revolting in equal measure.

'You no want this but I give you this. This my medal. It no winning medal like you desire but it good and I give you it for you and for this moment. It come for bottom of my heart.'

Emerson placed his runner-up medal into my hand and smiled. I looked at the medal, then looked at him. I took the medal and held it in my hands. The metal felt cool against my skin. I wrapped the lanyard around my wrist and let the medal drop, watching it as it dangled in mid-air, like some sort of magic. I smiled at Emerson Thome, and stroked his face gently. Then, without warning and in front of the rest of the team, I began to beat him brutally with his own medal. Even as his squeals of agony bounced off the walls of the otherwise silent dressing room, I continued with the sustained attack, beating him about the head and neck with reckless abandon. It was like Al Capone battering that shit-prick with a baseball bat in *The Untouchables*. Such was the ferocity of the onslaught, many of the other lads in the squad began to cry. Per Frandsen got so frightened, he actually soiled himself.

'*Ade due damballa!*' I screamed, as I continued to rain down blows upon the Brazilian braggart. 'Give me the power, I beg of you!'

'That's from *Child's Play,* isn't it, boss?' said perennial teacher's pet, Kevin Nolan, as he tucked into a packet of Wotsits with alarming nonchalance.

'Shut up, you tepid fucking quim, or you'll feel my wrath next!' I barked back.

When I was finished, Thorne was a bloody mess. He lay on the ground like a crimson puddle. I sold both him and Frandsen to Wigan Athletic a few months later. I couldn't look at either of them again after what had happened.

I left Wembley on my motorbike that afternoon, engulfed in a deep depression that had still not cleared three months later. By then, my blunting had started to become an issue. My energy sapped by melancholy, I would lie in my den all night, blazing blunts, staring at my lava lamp, and listening to every single record *Pitchfork* named in their Best New Music section. In my mind, the weed and the fresh jams were helping to dull the pangs of pain that jabbed mercilessly at my heart. In reality, though, they were nothing more than a crutch. Indeed, not even the magnificence of recently released *A Grand Don't Come for Free*, with its innovative narrative and sick rhymes, could yank me from the funk that was holding me prisoner.

As I lay on my beanbag in my den on a humid Sunday night in May, I couldn't help but wonder if I would ever feel good again. Then my phone rang.

Who could be calling me at this hour? I picked up my Nokia N-Gage and studied it. How the fuck can you see who is ringing you on this fucking contraption?

I thought. Finally, I found the answer button and pressed it.

'Hello?' I said welcomingly.

'All right you, you wee dafty ye,' said a gruff voice from the other end of the line. 'Wut are ye doing, playing wi' yer baws, aye?'

I broke into a smile as wide as Rihanna's forehead. It was Sir Alex Ferguson. My hero. My mentor. My muse. He always exaggerated his Glaswegian accent when I answered the phone to him. The fucking scamp. Why was he phoning me, though? The great man had led his Manchester United side to FA Cup glory at Wembley just 24 hours earlier, peerlessly seeing off Millwall's criminals with a sumptuous 3-0 victory. One would imagine that he'd be much too busy celebrating yet another trophy to have the time to call little old me.

This, however, was exactly the kind of mentality that made Sir Alex the winner he is. Once a trophy was in the bag, that was it. He didn't give it another thought. It was in the past and he immediately moved on to his next target, which, it soon transpired, was cheering up yours truly.

Sir Alex and I have a truly special bond. He has been my rock for almost two decades now, supporting me, protecting me, inspiring me. More than anyone else, he has helped weave the very fabric of my being. He is the ice cream beneath my cherry. The hummus to my breadstick. The Thom Yorke to my Colin Greenwood. Sir Alex sustains me, and when he graces me with a phone call, I'll sit up and listen.

It seemed the wily Scot had noticed how subdued I was at taekwondo class a few days earlier and was determined to get me out of my seemingly never-ending slump once and for all.

'Right, it's time you stopped wallowing,' he said, sternly. 'I'm getting you out of that fucking den of yours. Meet me at the skate park at Platt Fields tomorrow morning at 10 am. Bring your board. Leave your grumpy fucking fanny at home.'

I honestly felt some of the strain lift almost immediately. Sir Alex's words – even when he's scolding me or telling me what to do – have always soothed me, and the fact that he cared enough about me to call made me feel ten feet taller. It wasn't just a token either; he knew just what to say to make me feel better. I've had some of the greatest moments of my life skating with him, and I was already ecstatic about hitting the ramps with him the next day.

I travelled to Fallowfield, Manchester the next morning and rocked up to Platt Fields. Inevitably, Sir Alex was already there, doing his thing. Not a lot of people know this, but Sir Alex is an incredible skateboarder. I'm not ashamed to admit that he's infinitely better than me. While I'm certainly no slouch on the board, I'll never be able to marry elegance and aggression the way he can at a skate park. He's so much more than that, though. He's innovative. He's brave. He's magical.

He hadn't seen me, so I stood and watched him for a moment. He looked absolutely fucking adorable with his little helmet and knee pads. There wasn't anything adorable, however, about the totally fucking awesome frontside alley-oop he launched into. A move that had me whooping and hollering like an unhappy wife at her daughter's hen party.

'Stop gawping and get that curvy butt in here,' shouted Sir Alex mischievously when he spotted me. I didn't need a second invitation.

We skated for about an hour with not a single soul around apart from us. It was like we were the only people on the entire planet at that moment. The mists of misery were beginning to float away when I tried a Casper flip and fell down ungainly like a sack of wet shite. The newfound exhilaration I was experiencing was in danger of disappearing as quickly as it had arrived, but as I lay on the ground feeling humiliated, Sir Alex knelt down beside me, leaned close to my ear and whispered, 'Never fear hitting the ground, my rose, for only when a man has felt the earth beneath his feet can he truly fly amongst the clouds.'

I was stunned. A lesser person would have used the moment for cruel, derisive laughter or offered only some trite, half-arsed sympathy. Not Sir Alex, though. No matter what the situation, he analyses with the precision of a surgeon and offers the perfect retort. Winning football games might be his artistry, but his capacity for benevolence is his true masterpiece. He's the sweetest, most brilliant man I've ever met. I honestly think he might be Banksy as well.

I got straight up and began to skate again. In no time at all, I had regained my confidence and *joie de vivre*. I felt like I could do anything, and so I attempted a backside air. As I prepared to skate down the steep ramp, I looked over at Sir Alex. He was standing at the other side of the ramp, watching over me like a guardian angel. I was a little nervous, but the sheer serenity of his poise tranquillised me. When he started singing Cyndi Lauper's 'Time After Time', I was ready to skate off a fucking cliff.

I zoomed down the ramp at full speed and performed the most majestic backside air the skate park has ever seen. As I flew into the air, I felt all the sorrow and anguish I was drowning in for the past three months finally leave my body for good. 'I can touch the clouds, Sir Alex!' I squealed, with the unrestrained delight of a gay lad hearing some spiteful office gossip. 'I'm touching the clouds and I don't ever want to come down!'

Sir Alex chuckled, and shrugged insouciantly. 'You never have to, son,' he whispered. 'You never have to.'

I left the skate park imbued with a renewed sense of energy and hope. I decided to put a cap on my man-cave time, ditch the blunts and put all my strength into being the greatest manager Bolton Wanderers has ever seen. Was I successful in this endeavour? Well, the following season, I led the team to a sixth-place finish, qualifying for the UEFA Cup for the first time in the club's history. Does that sound like success to you? Answers on a cunting postcard.

As a society, we have been able to demolish many taboos that once seemed unassailable over the past century. Women are allowed to vote, the separation between church and state has become more pronounced and gay marriage is a protected institution in most developed countries. One thing civilisation still seems to have trouble with, however, is the very idea of platonic love existing between two men.

Even the most cursory of moments spent observing Sir Alex Ferguson and myself in each other's company, however, would destroy such tawdry bigotry instantly. To witness two men of such grandeur being so comfortable in expressing very real love for one another is not something that should make society blanch with embarrassment or disgust. It is something to cherish. Something to build upon.

During his 26 years as manager of Manchester United, Sir Alex Ferguson bestrode the game like a colossus; his tactical mastery matched only by his fearsome approach to battle and his granite-coated refusal to be beaten. Perhaps his greatest strength as a manager, however, was his ability to groom young, often wayward, men for world-class football. Not only did he teach them how to be winners, he taught them how to be men. I was obviously never fortunate enough to play under Sir Alex, but I remain arguably his most devoted pupil. His teachings have turned me into the manager I am today, his insights providing me with the platform to display my patented tactical virtuosity. He is the very areola beneath Big Sam's sensuous, rosebud nipples. Most importantly, though, Sir Alex Ferguson taught me how to love another man. He taught me how to appreciate the vulnerability in my fellow man and to see the beauty of the friendships that can arise from such susceptibility.

I don't see Sir Alex as much as I used to, following his retirement. I'll take him out to a funfair or for a walk around the shops once in a while, but our days of skateboarding are long gone. It doesn't matter, though. The memories we have made over the years will last a lifetime. The love we have shared can't be broken or tarnished or manipulated. After all these years, he can still make me giggle or cry with a single word. It can still feel like we're the only two people left on Earth when I'm with him. Our moments together may be fleeting these days, but they're still as magical as ever.

As my good, recently divorced, friend Mary recently said on Facebook, friends are like stars; you don't always see them, but you know they are there.

I love you Sir Alex Ferguson. Wherever you are.

# Epilogue

When I skidded effortlessly out of my mother's vagina all those years ago, never in my wildest dreams could I have imagined the journey ahead of me.

I had a wonderful career as a player, but it's as a manager that I truly believe I have made a lasting contribution to the world around me. The boys at Opta once told me that, according to their calculations, my innovations within the game have actually improved football in this country by 31.9 per cent. It's an incredible stat, whichever way you look at it, and one that I am immensely proud of.

Earlier this year I took the decision to leave Crystal Palace. Whether I am now in full retirement or just taking a well-earned sabbatical, I really don't know. But as I continue in my sixth decade on this planet, replete with titles, promotions, a 100 per cent win ratio as England manager and more Manager of the Month awards than you can shake an accusatory stick at, I ask myself, 'What more do you want to achieve?' It's a hard one to answer.

If I am being honest, though, it is the connections that I have made over the years that I hold dearest. The friendships. The fans. It is they that I count as my most valuable and treasured achievements. It is the people that I have touched, rather than the silverware.

I often describe myself as a jockey, splitting my time in the stable between two champion horses. One of the stallions is called Tactical Supremacy, and the other is called Human Compassion. Which of these mighty steeds would I rather win the Grand National with? Both of them. And none of them. Or just one of them. Any of them, to be honest.

At the end of the day, I am a storyteller. Whether that story is about qualifying for Europe with Bolton Wanderers or skateboarding with Sir Alex Ferguson, it really doesn't matter. It is the tapestry of tales that I weave and the wisdom found within those tales, that truly enables me to connect with people. With you.

I firmly believe that it is our ability to impart wisdom and comfort each other with stories that truly sets us apart from the animal kingdom. It's why we're better than monkeys and hippos and dolphins and always fucking will be. People say dolphins are dead clever, but have you ever seen one lead a team to the League of Ireland First Division title? Or have an entire room at an LMA function in fits of laughter with a perfectly delivered anecdote about Simon Weston, a tiny clown car and a circus flamethrower? Have you fuck.